Place

This edition first published 2015
© 2015 John Wiley & Sons Ltd
Edition history: Blackwell Publishing Ltd (1e, 2004)

Registered Office
John Wiley & Sons Ltd, The Atrium, Southern Gate, Chichester, West Sussex, PO19 8SQ, UK

Editorial Offices
350 Main Street, Malden, MA 02148-5020, USA
9600 Garsington Road, Oxford, OX4 2DQ, UK
The Atrium, Southern Gate, Chichester, West Sussex, PO19 8SQ, UK

For details of our global editorial offices, for customer services, and for information about how to apply for permission to reuse the copyright material in this book please see our website at www.wiley.com/wiley-blackwell.

The right of Tim Cresswell to be identified as the author of this work has been asserted in accordance with the UK Copyright, Designs and Patents Act 1988.

Library of Congress Cataloging-in-Publication Data
Cresswell, Tim.
  Place: an introduction / Tim Cresswell. – Second edition.
     pages cm
  Includes bibliographical references and index.
  ISBN 978-0-470-65562-7 (pbk.)
1. Human geography.   2. Geographical perception.   I. Title.
  GF50.C74 2015
  304.2'3–dc23
                                    2014018394

A catalogue record for this book is available from the British Library.

Cover image: Untitled, South East Spain, 2006, Ben Murphy. From the series *The Riverbed*. Copyright Ben Murphy 2014.

Set in 10.5/13 pt Minion Pro by Toppan Best-set Premedia Limited
Printed and bound in Malaysia by Vivar Printing Sdn Bhd

3   2017

For Yi-Fu Tuan

Contents

Figures

Acknowledgments

Thinking and writing about place has, for me, been an interactive activity for many years. I have been fortunate enough to have encountered some outstanding teachers as a student. These include Peter Jackson, Jacquie Burgess, Denis Cosgrove, Yi-Fu Tuan, and Robert Sack. They have all inspired me in different ways and I hope some of that inspiration is evident in this book. Now that I am a teacher myself I find myself increasingly indebted to students who have taken ideas and run with them in startling directions. They include Gareth Hoskins, Peter Adey, Bradley L. Garrett, Kimberley Peters, Craig Martin, Amy Cutler, Andre Novoa, terri moreau, Rupert Griffiths, Weiqiang Lin, and Laura Prazeres. In the years between the first edition and this edition I spent seven happy years at the Geography Department at Royal Holloway, University of London, which proved to be a remarkable site of intellectual endeavor for a cultural geographer such as myself. Landscape Surgery was a particularly wonderful arena to discuss ideas about place, landscape, mobility, material culture, and just about anything else a cultural geographer could wish for. I am more particularly indebted to Carol Jennings for her careful reading of this manuscript and many useful suggestions. Michael Brown is the true inventor of the word anachorism that appears in Chapter 6. Finally, many thanks to Gerry Pratt and Nick Blomley for the invitation to write the original version of this book and to the good people at Wiley-Blackwell for helping along the way. Justin Vaughan at Wiley-Blackwell has been consistently encouraging and has provided much needed prods in the years since I agreed to write the second edition.

Extracts from *Space, Place, and Gender* (1994) by Doreen Massey are used by permission of Polity Press, University of Minnesota Press, and the author.

Foreword

The first edition of *Place: A Short Introduction* was published in 2004 as part of a series of short introductions in geography. The idea was to focus on a concept rather than a traditional subfield. I had some doubt as to whether such a book would have a market as a teaching tool. While a concept such as place is clearly central to the discipline of geography – the discipline I was writing for and from – it is rarely the case that there is a course with place as its singular focus. I have been delighted, therefore, at the way the first edition has been used so widely both in geography and beyond. It was much more successful that I ever imagined. It certainly has been widely used as a text book in geography courses at both undergraduate and postgraduate level. What is more encouraging is the way it has been used across disciplines it was not explicitly aimed at. These include creative writing, English literature, American studies, religious studies, architecture, and interdisciplinary liberal arts. There are even courses with the title "place studies" that use it.

In addition to the obvious importance of place across a range of disciplines in the academy, there has been a resurgence of place issues in the wider world beyond. The events of the Arab Spring and Occupy were frequently framed around place issues. There have been lively discussions about the effects of multinationals and chain stores on the downtowns of cities. The idea of the local (a derivative of place) has been powerful in the rise of new-old forms of food culture and economic systems. Writing about place in the form of creative non-fiction has seen a renaissance in the United Kingdom (the place I know best) with place-based books appearing in national newspapers and in the bestseller lists. Art, too, has continued to ask questions of place and belonging.

Researching and writing about place, then, is clearly both an interdisciplinary endeavor and a practice that extends beyond the academy. For this reason the second edition of *Place: A Short Introduction* is a more interdisciplinary and outward-looking book, less focused on the discipline of geography. Geography has a lot to offer, thanks to its history of focusing on place, but it is not the sole owner of the concept. This is an offering, from the place of geography, to the wider world. This edition is about 50 percent longer than the first edition and, therefore, not so "short." I hope, nevertheless, to have maintained the accessibility of the first edition. In addition to a more generally interdisciplinary sense to the book, there are added sections which reflect the engagement with place across disciplines. These include sections on philosophy, architecture, art and place, information technologies, assemblage theory, and animal geographies amongst others. Otherwise encouraging notes from a few readers noted a number of errors in the first edition and I am grateful to them. I have kept a list and have hopefully rectified these issues.

1

Introduction: Defining Place

Place is one of the two or three most important terms for my discipline – geography. If pushed, I would argue that it is the most important of them all. Geography is about place and places. But place is not the property of geography – it is a concept that travels quite freely between disciplines and the study of place benefits from an interdisciplinary approach. Indeed, the philosopher Jeff Malpas (2010) has argued that "place is perhaps the key term for interdisciplinary research in the arts, humanities and social sciences in the twenty-first century."

This book is, therefore, both a disciplinary account of a key geographical concept and an interdisciplinary introduction to an issue that transcends geography, philosophy, or any other discipline. Regardless of the discipline we are rooted in, and despite this general enthusiasm for the study of places, there has been very little considered understanding of what the word "place" means. This is as true in theory and philosophy as it is among the new students signing up for university geography courses. Place is a word that seems to speak for itself.

Given geography's long history of grappling with the issue of place, the relatively recent resurgence in interest in place across disciplines and in the wider world presents an opportunity for geography to situate itself at the center of a lively interdisciplinary debate. Discussions of place are popping up everywhere. Creative writers and literary scholars have been busy rediscovering and "re-enchanting" place. In the English-speaking world there has been a resurgence in creative non-fiction which puts place at the heart of things. Writing on both "wild" and urban places has become more visible

Place: An Introduction, Second Edition. Tim Cresswell.
© 2015 John Wiley & Sons, Ltd. Published 2015 by John Wiley & Sons, Ltd.

with the popularity of forms of "psychogeography" and nature-writing (Sinclair 2009, Macfarlane 2007). A recent collection of essays and poems about places across Britain was titled *Towards Re-Enchantment: Place and Its Meanings* (Evans and Robson 2010). The text on the cover reads "Here are paths, offered like an open hand, towards a new way of being in the world, At a time when multiple alienations of modern society threaten our sense of belonging, the importance of 'place' to creative possibility in life and art cannot be underestimated." Artists, too, are grappling with place. Gstaad, in Switzerland, is a small alpine town visited regularly by the richest people in the world. It is a place for the 1 percent. Recently it was also the site of an array of artistic interventions by some of the world's leading conceptual artists. One of the installations, by the British artist Christian Marclay, is a video screen installed in a cable car which shows extracts from Bollywood movies which are set in the immediate vicinity. Gstaad, it turns out, is frequently used as a setting for escapist dream and dance sequences in Bollywood movies. The idea for the exhibition was Neville Wakefield's. Wakefield is a curator for the British art fair Frieze. His rationale for the project is outlined in an article in the *New York Times*.

> But the show…is also a response to their frustration with seeing so much art "set in these jewel box architectural spaces, and you really can't tell whether you are in Singapore, Shanghai, Berlin, London or whatever," Mr. Wakefield said, adding, "What's happened in terms of making art accessible is that it's homogenized."

Their exhibition, he said, is meant to be an antidote to the "art-fair, urban, white-cube gallery experience."

"It is difficult to get to," Mr. Wakefield added, "but because of that, it also demands a different kind of attention. You discover the art through the place and the place through the art" (Donadio 2014, C2).

The exhibition at Gstaad reflects a wider interest in how art and place interact on the part of both artists and art theorists (Doherty 2009, Hawkins 2010, Kwon 2002).

It is not just the creative world of writers and artists that are engaging place. At the other end of subjective–objective spectrum, place has also entered the lexicon of businesses and scholars who use geographic informa-tion systems (GIS). GIS are sophisticated computational software systems that can represent data spatially in the form of maps. Since their origin they have largely been centered on the manipulation and representation of concept of place and its centrality to both interdisciplinary academic endeavor and everyday life.

Think of the ways place is used in everyday speech. "Would you like to come round to my place?" This suggests ownership or some kind of connection between a person and a particular location or building. It also suggests a notion of privacy and belonging. "My place" is not "your place" – you and I have different places. "Brisbane is a nice place." Here "place" is referring to a city in a common-sense kind of way and the fact that it is nice suggests something of the way it looks and what it is like to be there. "She put me in my place" refers to more of a sense of position in a social hierarchy. "A place for everything and everything in its place" is another well-known phrase that suggests that there are particular orderings of things in the world that have a socio-geographical basis. Place is everywhere. This makes it different from other terms in geography like "territory," which announces itself as a specialized term, or "landscape" which is not a word that permeates through our everyday encounters. So what is this "place"?

Cast your mind back to the first time you moved into a particular space – a room in college accommodation is a good example. You are confronted with a particular area of floor space and a certain volume of air. In that room there may be a few rudimentary pieces of furniture such as a bed, a desk, a set of drawers and a closet. These are common to all the rooms in the complex. They are not unique and mean nothing to you beyond the provision of certain necessities of student life. Even these bare essentials have a history. A close inspection may reveal that a former owner has inscribed her name on the desk in an idle moment between classes. There on the carpet you notice a stain where someone has spilt some coffee. Some of the paint on the wall is missing. Perhaps someone had used putty to put up a poster. These are the hauntings of past inhabitation. This anonymous space has a history – it meant something to other people. Now what do you do? A common strategy is to make the space say something about you. You add your own possessions, rearrange the furniture within the limits of the space, put your own posters on the wall, arrange a few books purposefully on the desk. Thus space is turned into place. Your place.

The term 40.46°N 73.58°W does not mean much to most people. Some people with a sound knowledge of the globe may be able to tell you what this signifies but to most of us these are just numbers indicating a location – a site without meaning. These coordinates mark the location of New York City – somewhere south of Central Park in Manhattan. Immediately many images come into our heads. New York or Manhattan are place names rich

with meaning. We might think of skyscrapers, of 9/11, of shopping or of
any number of movie locations. Replacing a set of numbers with a name
means that we begin to approach "place." If we heard that two planes had
flown into 40.46°N 73.58°W it would not have quite the same impact as
hearing that they had flown into New York, into Manhattan, into the Twin
Towers. Cruise missiles are programmed with locations and spatial refer-
ents. If they could be programmed with "place" instead, with all the understanding that implies, they might decide to ditch in the desert.

Towards the southern tip of Manhattan and to the east of center is an
area – a place – known as the Lower East Side. This is an area which has
been known as a place of successive immigrant groups – Irish, Jewish,
German, Italian, Eastern European, Haitian, Puerto Rican, Chinese. It is a
little to the north of the infamous Five Corners – the setting for the film
The Gangs of New York (2002). It is a place of closely knit tenement blocks
south of Houston Street – buildings once crammed with large families in
small rooms. A succession of moral panics over immigration has focused
on this place. It has also been a place of political uprisings and police riots.
In the middle of this place is Tompkins Square Park, a little piece of nature
in the city built to provide a place of calm in the hurly burly of metropolitan
life. It was built in the 1830s and named after the US vice-president Daniel
Tompkins. Later the park became a place of demonstrations by unions and
anarchists as well as a place for children to play and the preaching of tem-
perance. By the 1960s it was the epicenter of a Lower East Side dominated
by bohemian counter-cultures, squatters and artists and by the 1980s it was
newly respectable – a place where the new cultural elite could savor city
life. Needless to say, property prices meant that the buildings were now out
of the reach of most people. Homeless people began to sleep in the park.
Some of the newly respectable residents were scared by this and supported
the removal of homeless people by the police. Once again, in 1986, the park
was the site of a demonstration and riot. In the area around the park, from
the 1960s on, residents were busy building 84 community gardens in vacant
lots. In 1997 Mayor Giuliani transferred responsibility for the gardens from
the City Parks Department to the Housing, Preservation and Development
Department with the intention that they be sold off for development. The
first four gardens were auctioned in July 1997 together with a local community center. In May 1999, 114 community gardens across New York were
saved from development when they were bought by Bette Midler's New
York Restoration Fund and Trust for Public Land for a combined total of
$4.2 million. However the policy of privatization has continued, and
gardens continued to be demolished.

Figure 1.2 A Manhattan community garden. These were built on vacant lots by local residents when the land had been abandoned by the government. When land became valuable the city government demolished many of these in the East Village in order to build apartments and parking lots. Source: the photo was taken by participant/team Corn Fed Chicks as part of the Commons:Wikis Take Manhattan project on October 4, 2008. Creative Commons Attribution-Share Alike 3.0 Unported license. http://creativecommons.org/licenses/by-sa/3.0 CC-BY-SA-3.0 Creative Commons Attribution-Share Alike 3.0 truetrue (Contributed by author) [CC-BY-SA-3.0 (http://creativecommons.org/licenses/by-sa/3.0)], via Wikimedia Commons.

If you visit the Lower East Side now you can dine in any number of fancy and not-so-fancy restaurants, bars and cafés, you can shop in boutiques and admire the brownstone architecture. You can stroll through Tompkins Square Park and visit the remaining community gardens. Crossing over Houston Street to the south you can visit the Lower East Side

Tenement Museum in one of the old buildings that formally housed new immigrants. You could, in other words, see many manifestations of "place." The museum is an attempt to produce a "place of memory" where the experiences of immigrants will not be forgotten. The gardens are the result of the efforts of immigrants and others to carve out a place from a little piece of Manhattan for their community to enjoy nature. Some of the community gardens – often the first to be leveled – are the sites of *casitas* – little houses made by the Puerto Rican community to replicate similar buildings from "home." They are draped with Puerto Rican flags and other symbols of elsewhere. Old men sit out in the sun watching baseball. Community meetings take place around these 8 ft × 10 ft buildings. They are, as the urban historian Delores Hayden puts it:

> a conscious choice by community organizers to construct the rural, preindustrial *bohío*…from the island as a new kind of community center in devastated tenement districts such as Lower Harlem, the South Bronx, and the Lower East Side…Painted in coral, turquoise, or lemon yellow, these dwellings recall the colors of the Caribbean and evoke a memory of the homeland for immigrants who find themselves in Alphabet City or Spanish Harlem. (Hayden 1995, 35–36)

Other gardens, ones not planted by Puerto Rican immigrants, are more bucolic, replicating some ideal of an English garden. Yet others are wild nature reserves set aside for local school lessons on biology and ecology. All of these are examples of the ongoing and diverse creation of places – sites of history and identity in the city.

Meanwhile back in Tompkins Square Park there are still tensions between the needs of the homeless to have even the smallest and most insecure "place for the night" and the desires of some local residents to have what they see as an attractive and safe place to live and raise families – one that does not include the homeless. Again places are being made, maintained, and contested. New York and Manhattan are places. The Lower East Side is a place. The Tenement Museum, community gardens, and Tompkins Square Park are all part of the rich tapestry of place-making that makes up the area in and around 40.46°N 73.58°W. We will return to the Lower East Side throughout the book to illustrate the many facets of the use of "place" in geography.

All over the world people are engaged in place-making activities. Home-owners redecorate, build additions, manicure the lawn. Neighborhood

Figure 1.3 Tompkins Square Park, New York City. Here sunbathers relax on the central knoll but this place has been the site of numerous protests and struggles. Source: photo by David Shankbone [CC-BY-SA-3.0 (http://creativecommons.org/ licenses/by-sa/3.0) or GFDL (http://www.gnu.org/copyleft/fdl.html)], via Wikimedia Commons.

organizations put pressure on people to tidy their yards; city governments legislate for new public buildings to express the spirit of particular places. Nations project themselves to the rest of the world through postage stamps, money, parliament buildings, national stadia, tourist brochures, etc. Within nation-states, oppressed groups attempt to assert their own identities. Just as the new student climbs on the bed to put the poster on the wall so the Kosovan Muslim flies a new flag, erects a new monument, and redraws the map. Graffiti artists write their tags in flowing script on the walls of the city. This is their place too.

So what links these examples: a child's room, an urban garden, a market town, New York City, Kosovo and the Earth? What makes them all places

Figure 1.4 St. Mark's Place in Manhattan's East Village. A busy shopping street full of boutiques, coffee shops, and other signs of a gentrified place. Source: photo by Beyond My Ken (own work) [GFDL (http://www.gnu.org/copyleft/fdl.html) or CC-BY-SA-3.0-2.5-2.0-1.0 (http://creativecommons.org/licenses/by-sa/3.0)], via Wikimedia Commons.

and not simply a room, a garden, a town, a world city, a new nation, and an inhabited planet? One answer is that they are all spaces which people have made meaningful. They are all spaces people are attached to in one way or another. This is the most straightforward and common definition of place – a meaningful location.

The political geographer John Agnew has outlined three fundamental aspects of place as a "meaningful location" (Agnew 1987):

1 location
2 locale
3 sense of place.

Figure 1.5 Graffiti on the Lower East Side, Manhattan. Some forms of place-making are less formal but are, nonetheless, important components in creating a sense of place. Source: photo by Summ (own work) [GFDL (http://www.gnu.org/copyleft/fdl.html), CC-BY-SA-3.0 (http://creativecommons.org/licenses/by-sa/3.0/) or CC-BY-SA-2.5-2.0-1.0 (http://creativecommons.org/licenses/by-sa/2.5-2.0-1.0)], via Wikimedia Commons.

Perhaps the most obvious point is that all of the places mentioned above are located. They have fixed objective coordinates on the Earth's surface (or in the Earth's case a specific location vis-à-vis other planets and the sun). New York is "here" and Kosovo is "there." Given the appropriate scale, we could find them on a map. The word place is often used in everyday language to simply refer to location. When we use place as a verb for instance (where should I place this?) we are usually referring to some notion of location – the simple notion of "where." But places are not always stationary. A ship, for instance, may become a special kind of place for people who share it on a long voyage, even though its location is constantly changing. By "locale" Agnew means the material setting for social relations – the actual shape of place within which people conduct their lives as individuals, as men or women, as white or black, straight or gay. It is clear that places almost always have a concrete form. New York is a collection of buildings and roads and public spaces including the community gardens which are themselves material – made of plants and statues and little sheds and houses with fences around them. The child's room has four walls, a window, a door, and a closet. Places then, are material things. Even imaginary places, like Hogwarts School in the Harry Potter novels, have an imaginary materiality of rooms, staircases, and tunnels that make the novel work. As well as being located and having a material visual form, places must have some relationship to humans and the human capacity to produce and consume meaning. By "sense of place" Agnew means the subjective and emotional attachment people have to place. Novels and films (at least successful ones) often evoke a sense of place – a feeling that we the reader/viewer know what it is like to "be there." We often have a sense of place about where we live, or where we lived when we were children. This is what the author Lucy Lippard has called *The Lure of the Local* (Lippard 1997). It is commonplace in Western societies in the twenty-first century to bemoan a loss of a sense of place as the forces of globalization have eroded local cultures and produced homogenized global spaces. We will return to this issue of "placelessness" in Chapter 3.

We can see this combination of location, locale, and sense of place in the account of the Lower East Side. We could repeat this exercise anywhere. Latitude 51°30′18″ N Longitude 0°1′9″ W is a location but London's Dock-lands is a place. While they share the same objective position, London Docklands is a place that includes Canary Wharf, a Docklands Museum, office blocks, smart restaurants, and a light rail line. Like the Lower East Side and East Village, this place has a past. In this case it is a working-class and immigrant past associated with the docks and with slavery. It is part of my past. My maternal grandmother lived there before she was evacuated with her children in World War II. The street she lived on no longer exists. Outside of the museum, very little of the past is apparent in this shiny new glass and steel place. You have to work hard to find it. As well as being a location, then, this place, like any place, has a physical landscape (buildings, infrastructure, etc.) and a "sense of place" – meanings, both personal and shared, that are associated with a particular locale.

Agnew's three-part definition of place certainly accounts for most examples of place. In addition, however, it helps to think of place in distinction to two other familiar concepts – "space" and "landscape" – both of which are occasionally substituted with the word "place."

Space and Place

An advertisement for a large furniture shop in my Sunday paper read "Transforming space into place." Such an advertisement cannot rely on an in-depth understanding of the development of the concept of place and yet it speaks to one of the central themes in work on place. The ad suggests that we might want to take the rooms we have recently bought or rented and make them mean something to us by arranging furniture in them – making them comfortable literally and experientially. Humanistic geographers are unlikely to agree that the mere purchase of furniture is going to enact such a transformation but they will recognize the intent.

Space is a more abstract concept than place. When we speak of space we tend to think of outer-space or the spaces of geometry. Spaces have areas and volumes. Places have space between them. Yi-Fu Tuan has likened space to movement and place to pauses – stops along the way.

> What begins as undifferentiated space becomes place as we get to know it better and endow it with value…The ideas "space" and "place" require each other for definition. From the security and stability of place we are aware of the openness, freedom, and threat of space, and vice versa. Furthermore, if we think of space as that which allows movement, then place is pause; each pause in movement makes it possible for location to be transformed into place. (Tuan 1977, 6)

Consider the relationship between the sea and land along the coast between Seattle and Vancouver. In his book *Passage to Juneau* the travel writer Jonathan Raban tells of his trip by boat along that shore (Raban 1999). Alongside his travel narrative he tells of the voyage of the explorer Captain Vancouver in his ship HMS *Discovery* in 1792. Vancouver's task was to map the coast and name it as he went – making it a place of empire. Naming is one of the ways space can be given meaning and become place. Vancouver's journal reports the seemingly nonsensical movements of natives in their canoes in the sea around them. Rather then taking a direct line from point A to point B the natives would take complicated routes that had no apparent logic. To the native canoeists their movements made perfect sense as they read the sea as a set of places associated with particular spirits and particular dangers. While the colonialists looked at the sea and saw blank space, the natives saw place.

Two world-views were in collision; and the poverty of white accounts of these canoe journeys reflects the colonialists' blindness to the native sea. They didn't get it – couldn't grasp the fact that for Indians the water was a place, and the great bulk of the land was undifferentiated space.

The whites had entered a looking-glass world, where their own most basic terms were reversed. Their whole focus was directed toward the land: its natural harbours, its timber, its likely spots for settlement and agriculture. They travelled everywhere equipped with mental chainsaws and at a glance could strip a hill of its covering forest…and see there a future of hedges, fields, houses, churches. They viewed the sea as a medium of access to the all-important land.

Substitute "sea" for "land" and vice-versa, in that paragraph, and one is very close to the world that emerges from Indian stories, where the forest is the realm of danger, darkness, exile, solitude, and self-extinction, while the sea and its beaches represent safety, light, home, society, and the continuation of life. (Raban 1999, 103)

Raban recounts the visit of the German geographer Aurel Krause while working for the Breman Geographical Society in 1881. He was astonished by what he saw as the local Tlingits' ignorance of their place in the world, which to him was dominated by the enormous mountains that towered behind the small strip of land they inhabited beside the sea.

In spite of the fact that the Tlingit is constantly surrounded by nature, he is only acquainted with it as it offers him the necessities of life. He knows every bay that lends itself to fishing or the beaching of a canoe…and for these he has names; but the mountain peaks themselves, even though they are out-standing on account of their shape and size, are scarcely noticed by him. (Raban 1999, 106)

The Tlingits had many names for the sea, but the land remained unnamed and seemingly invisible. To the explorers the sea was empty space and the land full of potential places waiting to be mapped and named, but this was the mirror image of the Tlinget "sense of place."

Space, then, has been seen in distinction to place as a realm without meaning – as a "fact of life" which, like time, produces the basic coordinates for human life. When humans invest meaning in a portion of space and then become attached to it in some way (naming is one such way) it becomes a place. Although this basic dualism of space and place runs through much of human geography since the 1970s it is confused somewhat by the idea of social space – or socially produced space – which, in many ways, plays the same role as place (Lefebvre 1991).

Place and Landscape

Another concept that frequently appears alongside place is landscape. The idea of landscape has a very particular history which dates back to the emergence of mercantile capitalism in Renaissance Venice and Flanders. Landscape painting emerged with the rediscovery of the science of optics, new techniques of navigation, and the development of a new class of traders. Landscape referred to a portion of the earth's surface that can be viewed from one spot (Cosgrove 1984, Jackson 1997). It combined a focus on the material topography of a portion of land (that which can be seen) with the notion of vision (the way it is seen). Landscape is an intensely visual idea. In most definitions of landscape the viewer is outside of it. This is the primary way in which it differs from place. Places are very much things to be inside of. Again a literary example illustrates this.

In Raymond Williams's (1960) novel *Border Country*, Matthew Price returns to the place of his childhood in the Welsh borders after spending many years at university in England. He is surprised at what he finds when he gets there. He has forgotten the qualities of life that made it a "place" and replaced it in his mind with a "landscape." What follows is an examination of the gap between the idea of the village as "landscape" and the idea of the village as a lived and felt "place." As Matthew realizes he has become an outsider in his own village he reflects on his change of perspective:

> He realized as he watched what had happened in going away. The valley as landscape had been taken, but its work forgotten. The visitor sees beauty, the inhabitant a place where he works and has his friends. Far away, closing his eyes, he had been seeing this valley, but as the visitor sees it, as the guide book sees it. (Williams 1960, 75)

Later in the novel Matthew gets back into the routine of the village "It was no longer a landscape or view, but a valley that people were using." No longer a view from a hill, the valley was once again a place. Landscape refers to the shape – the material topography – of a piece of land. This may be apparently natural landscape (though few, if any, parts of the Earth's surface are untouched by humans) or it might be the obviously human, or cultural, landscape of a city. We do not live in landscapes – we look at them.

Place as a Way of Understanding

An important theme of this book is that place is not just a thing in the world but a way of understanding the world. While we hold common-sense ideas of what places are, these are often quite vague when subjected to critical reflection. Most often the designation of place is given to something quite small in scale, but not too small. Neighborhoods, villages, towns, and cities are easily referred to as places and these are the kinds of places that most often appear in writing on place. There is little writing on the corner of a favorite room as place at one scale, or on the globe at another. Yet, as Tuan suggested, there is something of place in all of these. So, as it turns out, places as "things" are quite obscure and hard to grasp.

But place is also a way of seeing, knowing, and understanding the world. When we look at the world as a world of places, we see different things. We see attachments and connections between people and place. We see worlds of meaning and experience. Sometimes this way of seeing can seem to be an act of resistance against a rationalization of the world that focuses more on space than place. To think of an area of the world as a rich and complicated interplay of people and the environment – as a place – is to free us from thinking of it as facts and figures. To think of Baghdad as a place is in a different world to thinking of it as a location on which to drop bombs. At other times, however, seeing the world through the lens of place leads to reactionary and exclusionary xenophobia, racism, and bigotry. "Our place" is threatened and others have to be excluded. Here "place" is not so much a quality of things in the world as an aspect of the way we choose to think about it – what we decide to emphasize and what we decide to designate as unimportant. This book is as much about place as a way of knowing as it is about place as a thing in the world. It is as much about epistemology as it is about ontology.

The Remainder of the Book

Space, landscape, and place are clearly highly interrelated terms and each definition is contested. The French urban theorist Henri Lefebvre, for instance, has produced a much more sophisticated account of space in which he distinguishes between more abstract kinds of space (absolute space) and lived and meaningful spaces (social space) (Lefebvre 1991). Social space is clearly very close to the definition of place. We will return to debates such as this as we consider the intellectual trajectory of place in the next chapter. For now it suffices to say that the majority of writing about place focuses on the realm of meaning and experience. Place is how we make the world meaningful and the way we experience the world. Place, at a basic level, is space invested with meaning in the context of power. This process of investing space with meaning happens across the globe at all scales, and has done throughout human history. It has been one of the central tasks of human geography to make sense of it.

This introduction has provided some provisional outlines of what place means. But this is just a starting point. If it were that easy I could stop now. The fact is that place is a contested concept and what it is that "place" means is very much the subject of decades of debate in human geography as well as philosophy, planning, architecture, and any number of other disciplines. To some in planning, place refers to the built environment. To ecologists, a place is rooted in a distinctive ecology – as a bioregion. To a philosopher, place is a way of being-in-the-world. The rest of this book is an extended investigation of what place means and how the concept has been and might be used across disciplines and in the wide world beyond.

To that end the remainder of this book is organized as follows. Chapter 2 traces the development of place as a concept, drawing largely on work in philosophy and geography. It situates the philosophical origins of the concept of place in Greek philosophy and sketches its trajectory to the present day, showing how place became a central term in North American geography during the late 1970s and early 1980s through the efforts of primarily humanistic geographers (Relph 1976, Tuan 1974). It traces the roots of this engagement back to the philosophies of meaning – particularly those of Heidegger and Merleau-Ponty. The chapter also accounts for the appropriation of the term by cultural geography, and the linking of place to politics and arguments over who gets to define the meaning of a place (Cresswell 1996). Chapter 3 considers the role of place in relation to mobility. We live in an increasingly mobile world and this has led some to describe increasing "placelessness" due to the effects of "time–space compression" (Augé 1995, Harvey 1989). Chapter 3 interrogates this idea through an exploration of the many ways in which mobility and place constitute each other, including accounts of the way senses of place are

constructed through bodily mobilities in place (Seamon 1980), Doreen
Massey's conception of a "progressive sense of place" (Massey 1997) and
anthropological accounts of cosmopolitanism and "friction" (Tsing 2005,
Hannerz 1990).

Chapter 4 consists of a critical evaluation of Doreen Massey's paper "A
global sense of place" (Massey 1997). Massey's paper has been widely cited
as a plea for a new conceptualization of place as open and hybrid – a
product of interconnecting flows – of routes rather then roots. This extroverted notion of place calls into question the whole history of place as a
center of meaning connected to a rooted and "authentic" sense of identity
forever challenged by mobility. It also makes a critical intervention into the
widely held notions of time–space compression and the erosion of place
through globalization. In this chapter Massey's paper is contrasted with a
chapter by David Harvey which tackles similar issues in a very different
way (Harvey 1996) and a paper by Jon May which mobilizes these understandings in a detailed piece of research into a particular place (May 1996).

Chapters 5 and 6 focus on examples of ways in which the concept of
place has been mobilized in research, across disciplines and in the world
beyond. Chapter 5 concerns the way people have created places. These
include the idea of *genius loci* and the development of place in architecture;
the way memory and place intersect in the production of heritage places
such as museums; how particular visions of place are created in order to
get people to live there; the relationship between art and place, and the role
of place in the digital world. But places are not just small and local. Regions
and nations are also places and some geographers have looked at the production of place at a larger scale. These examples reveal how the concept
of place can still have salience in the contemporary world in widely diver-
gent contexts. Chapter 6 concerns the use of notions of appropriate place
to construct normative "moral geographies" that map particular kinds of
people and practice to particular places. Here I draw on my own work on
transgression in *In Place/Out of Place* (Cresswell 1996) and work on "people
without place," such as the homeless and refugees, as well as how gay,
lesbian and bisexual people are made to feel "out of place." Places are not
just about people. Other living things form part of place and these too can
be experienced as transgressive. The chapter also considers the role of place
in animal geographies. This work shows how place is used in the construction of ideas about who and what belong where and when, and thus in the
construction of those seen as "deviant" and outside of "normal" society.
While both of these sets of examples concern the connections between

place, identity, and power, they use place in radically different ways and from different political perspectives.

Finally, in Chapter 7, I provide an annotated bibliography as well as lists of key readings and texts, and a survey of web resources, pedagogical resources, and possible student projects.

References

Agnew, J. A. (1987) *Place and Politics: The Geographical Mediation of State and Society*. Boston, Allen & Unwin.

Augé, M. (1995) *Non-Places: Introduction to an Anthropology of Supermodernity*. London and New York, Verso.

Cosgrove, D. E. (1984) *Social Formation and Symbolic Landscape*. London, Croom Helm.

Cresswell, T. (1996) *In Place/Out of Place: Geography, Ideology and Transgression*. Minneapolis, University of Minnesota Press.

Doherty, C. (2009) *Situation*. Cambridge, MA, MIT Press.

Donadio, R. (2014) Artists go to town on a picturesque Swiss village. *New York Times*, 1 February 2014, p. C2.

Evans, G. and Robson, D. (2010) *Towards Re-enchantment: Place and Its Meanings*. London, Artevents.

Hannerz, U. (1990) Cosmopolitans and locals in world culture. *Theory, Culture and Society* 7, 237–251.

Harvey, D. (1989) *The Condition of Postmodernity*. Oxford.

Harvey, D. (1996) *Justice, Nature and the Geography of Difference*. Cambridge, Mass., Blackwell Publishers.

Hawkins, H. (2010) The argument of the eye: Cultural geographies of installation art. *Cultural Geographies* 17, 1–19.

Hayden, D. (1995) *The Power of Place: Urban Landscapes as Public History*. Cambridge, Mass., MIT Press.

Jackson, J. B. (1997) *Landscape in Sight: Looking at America*. New Haven, CT, Yale University Press.

Kimmelman, M. (2011) In protest: The power of place. *New York Times*, 15 October 2011, p. SR1.

Kwon, M. (2002) *One Place after Another: Site-Specific Art and Locational Identity*. Cambridge, Mass., MIT Press.

Lefebvre, H. (1991) *The Production of Space*. Oxford, Blackwell.

Lippard, L. (1997) *The Lure of the Local: Senses of Place in a Multicultural Society*. New York, The New Press.

Macfarlane, R. (2007) *The Wild Places*. London, Granta.

Malpas, J. E. (2010) *Progressive Geographies*. Available at http://progressive geographies.com/2010/11/04/place-research-network/ (accessed 28 May 2014).

Massey, D. (1997) A global sense of place, in *Reading Human Geography*, ed. T. Barnes and D. Gregory. London, Arnold, pp. 315–323.

May, J. (1996) Globalization and the politics of place: place and identity in an inner London neighbourhood. *Transactions of the Institute of British Geographers* 21, 194–215.

Raban, J. (1999) *Passage to Juneau: A Sea and Its Meanings*. New York, Pantheon Books.

Relph, E. (1976) *Place and Placelessness*. London, Pion.

Seamon, D. (1980) Body–subject, time–space routines, and place-ballets, in *The Human Experience of Space and Place*, ed. A. Buttimer and D. Seamon. London, Croom Helm, pp. 148–165.

Sinclair, I. (2009) *Hackney, That Rose-Red Empire: A Confidential Report*. London, Hamish Hamilton.

Sui, D. and Goodchild, M. (2011) The convergence of GIS and social media: Challenges for GIScience. *International Journal of Geographical Information Science* 25, 1737–1748.

Tsing, A. L. (2005) *Friction: An Ethnography of Global Connection*. Princeton, N.J., Princeton University Press.

Tuan, Y.-F. (1974) Space and place: Humanistic perspective. *Progress in Human Geography* 6, 211–252.

Tuan, Y.-F. (1977) *Space and Place: The Perspective of Experience*. Minneapolis, University of Minnesota Press.

Williams, R. (1960) *Border Country*. London, Chatto and Windus.

Wroclawski, S. (2014) Why the world needs OpenStreetMap. *The Guardian*, 14 January 2014. Online. Available at www.theguardian.com/technology/2014/jan/14/why-the-world-needs-openstreetmap (accessed 2 May 2014).

Zook, M. A. and Graham, M. (2007) Mapping DigiPlace: Geocoded Internet data and the representation of place. *Environment and Planning B-Planning and Design* 34, 466–482.

2

The Genealogy of Place

Place has been a constant theme in the history of Western thought since at least the first century AD. Geography, as a discipline, has only existed in a formal sense since the nineteenth century. To explore the genealogy of place as a concept and theme in intellectual endeavor it is thus necessary to consider place as a philosophical object of enquiry as well as a geographical one. Place, as we have already established, is an interdisciplinary issue. While this chapter focuses primarily on the disciplines of philosophy and geography, we will see later (in Chapter 5) how place has been at the heart of discussions of art, architecture, literature, history, anthropology, and a host of other disciplines (Low and Lawrence-Zuniga 2002, Kwon 2002, Prieto 2013, Feld and Basso 1996). Anthropologists explore the connections between place and identity. Architects and urban planners try to evoke senses of place in their practice and writing. Ecologists and green activists talk of ecological places they call "bioregions." Artists and writers attempt to reconstitute or challenge places in their work.

Despite the widespread and interdisciplinary nature of discussion of place, it is a concept that hides many differences. One confusing aspect of the genealogy of place is that place stands for both an object (a thing that we can look at, research, and write about) and a way of looking. Looking at the world as a set of places, in some way separate from each other, is both an act of defining what exists (ontology) and a particular way of seeing and knowing the world (epistemology and metaphysics). Theory is a way of looking at the world and making sense of the confusion of the senses. Different theories of place lead different writers to look at different

Place: An Introduction, Second Edition. Tim Cresswell.

aspects of the world. In other words, place is not simply something to be observed, researched, and written about but is itself part of the way we see, research, and write. Towards the end of this chapter we will see how geographers and philosophers have sought to show how place is a way-of-being. Here, place is deeply metaphysical and a long way from the simple distinction between one place and another.

Before embarking on our exploration of place as a concept, it is worth pausing to think about what is meant by the term "interdisciplinary." The philosopher J. E. Malpas, in his discussion of place, uses the term "interdisciplinary" in a guarded way. He does not mean to embrace a kind of featureless mélange of place research without disciplines. Rather, he recognizes that place research needs its own topography – that an interdisciplinary engagement with place benefits from having its own places from which place is theorized and written. These places are disciplines.

> Greater engagement across disciplines is no bad thing, of course, and one can certainly argue that we need more cross-fertilization between disciplines rather than less. Yet real productivity tends to emerge out of difference, and disciplinary difference requires a capacity for disciplines to be able to reflect upon and engage in articulation of the concepts and modes of thinking that give them their shape and character. (Malpas n.d.)

Malpas approaches interdisciplinarity as a field marked by places – locations with "shape and character" that enable us to have a conversation about place. I approach this conversation from the "place" of geography. I believe geography has a privileged relationship to the concept of place as there is no other discipline that has held place to be a central defining concept in the way geography has. The history of geography has taken as one of its central objects the common-sense experienced differences between portions of the Earth's surface. As Carl Sauer wrote in his seminal paper "The morphology of landscape," "the facts of geography are place facts" (Sauer and Leighly 1963, 321). Or as Richard Hartshorne wrote in *Perspectives on the Nature of Geography*, "The integrations which geography is concerned to analyze are those which vary from place to place" (Hartshorne 1959, 159). A quarter of a century later, Allan Pred asserted "[S]ettled places and regions, however arbitrarily defined, are the essence of human geographical inquiry" (Pred 1984, 279). There is probably not much that these three geographers would agree on but they could agree on the importance of place to the subject of geography. Philosophers, anthropologists, literary theorists, and others have had much to say about place, but only as one among many themes. No one would say that place was the central theme of philosophy, for instance. There is no way of accounting for all the richness of approaches to place across disciplines, so this chapter is simply an outline and a framework that I hope will encourage further exploration and interdisciplinary dialogue. This chapter is broadly arranged chronologically to give a sense of the historical progression of an idea. Towards the end however there are many competing definitions of and approaches to place that exist simultaneously. The starting point, however, is the emergence of place in Greek philosophy.

The Emergence of Place in Western Thought

The origins of geography are entangled with the origins of Western philosophy in Greek thought. Scholars such as Eratosthenes and Herodotus were geographers, philosophers, historians, and anthropologists before these disciplines even existed. In their different ways they sought to explore the "inhabited earth" – an idea encapsulated in the Greek term *oikoumene* (later, *ecumene*). They traveled, explored, measured, and reported back – defining one area of the world as different from the next due to the unique ways in which people and nature interacted to form specific and varied places (Cresswell 2013). These reports provided gazetteers of places. They were not investigations into the idea of place itself.

The first explicit philosophy of place emerged from the work of Plato and Aristotle, both of whom gave place a particularly powerful position in the lexicon of ideas. Their terms *chora* and *topos* broadly described what we might now think of as region and place. *Chora* is the root of chorology (the study of regions) and *topos* is at the root of topography and topology. Plato was interested in how things come into being – how nothing becomes something. To exist, he argued, something has to be differentiated from the void (*kenon* – which we might think of as one formulation of limitless and abstract space). Plato introduced the term *chora* to refer to a limited extent in space that is a kind of receptacle or container that has content within it – unlike *kenon*. *Topos* refers to an achieved place – the product of a process of becoming. In Aristotle, *chora* was broadly equated with a large region of country while *topos* would describe a smaller scale place within it (Casey 1998).

Aristotle held place to be the fundamental basis of existence for anything else. His logic was that for something to exist it had to be somewhere – "because what is not is nowhere – where for instance is a goat-stag or a sphinx?"(Aristotle in Casey 1998, 51). In this sense place (in the limited sense of location and container) has to come first ontologically – it is the ground for existence itself. For something to exist it has to be some place – so place, necessarily, provides the basis for existence.

The philosopher Edward Casey has written extensively about the idea of place in the history of philosophy. In his book *The Fate of Place*, for instance, he recounts the power that place had in early Greek philosophy and how an idea of place was gradually submerged under a rise in thought about space as a seemingly more analytic and universal concept (Casey 1998). There were certainly aspects of thinking about place that appeared in the work of philosophers between Greek philosophy and the twentieth century. One important figure, for instance, was Albertus Magnus (1193–1280). Albertus was an important translator of Aristotle and he inherited many of Aristotle's ideas about place. Among his many volumes, which straddled philosophy and the natural sciences, was *De Natura Locorum* (*The Nature of Places*). In this volume Albertus insists that the particularity of place plays a role in the kind of human life that develops in that place. A place, to Albertus, was a unique combination of cosmological and environmental influences that shapes the things that exist in that place. This view often took the form of what we could now call environmental determinism – the view that environmental factors such as climate and topography directly determine human character. This view became particularly powerful at the end of the nineteenth and in the early twentieth century. It formed the basis for all kinds of beliefs that we now see as racist. Albertus, for instance, believed that "Men born in stony, flat, cold, dry places are extremely strong and bony; their joints are plainly visible; they are of great stature, skilled in war and handy in waging it, and they have bony limbs" (Albertus quoted in Glacken 1967, 169). Albertus's beliefs about the importance of place were not, however, limited to place's influence on people. Everything basically belonged to a place and moving away from that place would weaken that thing – whether human, animal, vegetable or mineral. In his volume *De Mineralibus* (*Book of Minerals*), Albertus accounts for different kinds of rock with reference to their place or origin (the conditions that produced them) and then argues that a rock moved away from its place of origin becomes a weaker rock. Here place takes a metaphysical turn. It is an early example of a sedentarist metaphysics – a set of beliefs that sees place and

It also reflects a history of geography which had seen its practitioners focusing largely on the description of "regions." Much of human geography before the 1960s was devoted to specifying and describing the differences between areas of the Earth's surface. This "regional geography" was ideographic which is to say that it reveled in the particular. Why was the South of the United States different from the North? How many regions could be identified in England? The central word was region rather than place. The characteristic mode of operation for regional geographers was to describe a place/region in great detail, starting with the bedrock, soil type, and climate and ending with "culture." A great deal of time was spent differentiating one particular region from others around it – in other words, in drawing boundaries. Some geographers referred to this practice as "chorology" a spatial version of "chronology." While chronology refers to the study of time, chorology refers to the study of regions/places. The origins of chorology date back to the Greek geographer Strabo (first century AD) who described it as the description of the parts of the earth. The case for geography as chorology has been argued by Richard Hartshorne (Hartshorne 1939). Hartshorne was less interested in providing empirical accounts of particular places (regions) and more interested in thinking about what geography as a discipline had as its object. To Hartshorne, geography was about how things coalesce in a particular region.

> [Geography] interprets the realities of areal differentiation of the world as they are found, not only in terms of the differences of things from place to place, but also in terms of the total combination of phenomena in each place, different from those in every other place. (Hartshorne 1939, 462)

Hartshorne's account of the "nature of geography" attempted to provide a philosophical basis for the practice of regional geography. He established geography as an idiographic discipline – one which focuses on the unique and particular. This approach to geography, one often re-articulated in the years since 1939, resonates with contemporary philosophical approaches to place as a site of gathering or as an assemblage (Casey 1996). We will return to this theme later.

One influential tradition in human geography was the French tradition of *la géographie humaine* associated with Paul Vidal de la Blache at the end of the nineteenth and beginning of the twentieth century. Although the word place was not its central object, its focus on *genre de vie* (ways of life) in particular regions produced work which was remarkable in the way it captured the complicated interplay of the natural and cultural worlds in particular parts of France. *La géographie humaine* succeeded in emphasizing the distinctiveness of particular places in a way which later inspired humanistic geographers (Buttimer 1971, Ley 1977, Vidal de la Blache 1908).

Early American cultural geographers also used the term "region" in their descriptive work on the cultural landscape. In the influential text-book *Readings in Cultural Geography* (Wagner and Mikesell 1962), the editors present what they saw as the main themes in American cultural geography in 1962. The central figure in the text is Carl O. Sauer who had, like Vidal, rejected the simplistic determinism of the environmental determinists such as Ellen Semple and Ellsworth Huntingdon who had argued that the characteristics of human settlement (culture) were largely a response to environmental imperatives. In other words, environment determined society and culture. Rather than seeing culture as determined by the natural environment, Sauer and his followers asserted the importance of culture in transforming the natural environment. In the work of both Vidal and Sauer culture is given explanatory power. It is no longer simply a result of natural forces. The key themes Wagner and Mikesell identify as central to cultural geography are culture, culture area, cultural landscape, cultural history, and cultural ecology. Culture, they argue, rests on a geographical basis in that "habitual and shared communication is likely to occur only among those who occupy a common area" (Wagner and Mikesell 1962, 3). Cultural geography, therefore, rested on the ranking and classifying of "culture areas" (these spaces of cultural communication) and an analysis of the ways in which cultural groups affect and change their natural habitats. Again "place" is not a central concept here but the emphasis on shared cultural spaces suggests the importance of meaning and practice in a given location.

Regional geography was the predominant way of doing geography in Britain during the first half of the twentieth century. Approaches ranged from the attempts by Herbertson to show how unique regions emanated from variations in the natural environment (Herbertson 1905) to Fleure's equally ambitious desire to delineate "human regions" defined by the anthropological particularities of their inhabitants (Fleure 1919 [1996)). In each case the focus was on differentiating one clearly defined region (place) from the next and explaining the logic of the definitions. While Herbertson looked to nature for this logic, Fleure looked to human characteristics.

The importance of regions as places is a theme that still warrants the attention of geographers. More recently, geographers have explored the way regions have been deliberately produced through the activities of formal and informal politics in order to institutionalize particular ideas about government and governance at regional levels. Here the focus is very much on the social and political production of regions rather than the search for regions that already exist (Paasi 2002, Jones and MacLeod 2004). A different argument is made by Nick Entrikin as he traces some of the strands of thought in North America which have argued that the stability of democracy is based on an attachment to place and local community (Entrikin 1991). Such "sectionalism" would, it was hoped, mitigate "mass society." Such views were clearly held by Carl Sauer in his defense of traditional ways of life in the face of modern industrialism. To Sauer, an ecologically informed naturalistic philosophy pointed towards the increasing diversity of forms of living, with each community becoming recognizably separate. Activities and forms of human life and culture which threatened regional and place-based distinctiveness were thus a threat. In the conclusion to his book, *The Betweenness of Place*, Entrikin suggests that scientific geography – and the fascination with abstract space – had diminished the importance of the particular and that the particular needs to be reclaimed through a narrative understanding of place (Entrikin 1991).

Forms of regional geography continue to be influential. Some have attempted to reformulate a regional geography by arguing for a relational conception of the region (Amin 2004). We will see, through later chapters, how relational approaches to geography have redefined place. There has also been a limited attempt to account for individual places in ways that hark back to regional geography but are informed by more recent theoretical trajectories. We will return to these at the end of this chapter.

Discovering Place: Humanistic Geography

Given this history and the comments of Sauer, Hartshorne, and others, it is, as Edward Relph was to remark in 1976 in his book *Place and Placelessness*, surprising that very little attempt had been made to actually define place and distinguish it from its sister concepts of region and area. Place remained a largely common-sense idea. Perhaps the most insistent attempt to come to terms with the concept in the 1960s was made by Fred Lukerman. Echoing the earlier comments of Sauer and Hartshorne, Lukerman had argued that "Geography is the knowledge of the world as it exists in places" (Lukerman 1964, 167). Lukerman understood places as integrations of nature and culture developing in particular locations with links to other places through the movement of goods and people. This understanding of place is suggestive but also evasive. The words "culture" and "nature" are, as Raymond Williams has reminded us, two of the most complicated words in the English language, each of which has many possible meanings (Williams 1985). This definition hardly applies to the corner of a child's room. It also remains unclear how place might be different from area, locality, or territory.

Lukerman's interventions aside, the 1970s had not proved promising for the development of a thorough understanding of place. It was largely in this decade that geographers became dissatisfied with geography as an ideographic pursuit. Proper scientific disciplines, it was pointed out, liked to generalize and make laws that could be applicable anywhere – not just in Southern California or the South of France. Thus spatial science was born and the concept of region was replaced by the concept of space as a central focus of human geography. The term space appeals to the nomothetic or generalizing impulse of science. Within spatial science a place was simply a location. Central place theory was the only area in which the term "place" was often used and here it described locations where particular functions, services and populations were concentrated (Lösch 1954, Christaller 1966 [1933]).

As Arturo Escobar has noted:

> Since Plato, Western philosophy – often times with the help of theology and physics – has enshrined space as the absolute, unlimited and universal, while banning place to the realm of the particular, the limited, the local and the bound. (Escobar 2001, 143)

Since the particular had no place in the hierarchy of values developed in the post-Enlightenment world, studies of place were often relegated to "mere description" while space was given the role of developing scientific law-like generalizations. In order to make this work people had to be removed from the scene. Space was not embodied but empty. This empty space could then be used to develop a kind of spatial mathematics – a geometry. But this idea of place as a fascination with the particular and the study of place as "mere description" depends on a particular naïve view of places as given parts of the human landscape. It also depends on an equally naïve view of space as unpeopled and removed from society. In the 1970s humanistic geographers began to develop notions of place which were every bit as universal and theoretically ambitious as approaches to space had been.

The development of humanistic geography was, in part, a reaction to the new emphasis on space in spatial science. Central to this enterprise was "place" which, for the first time, explicitly became the central concept in geographical inquiry. Place, to geographers such as Yi-Fu Tuan (Tuan 1974a, 1977), Anne Buttimer, and David Seamon (Buttimer and Seamon 1980) and Edward Relph (1976) was a concept that expressed an attitude to the world that emphasized subjectivity and experience rather than the cool, hard logic of spatial science. But unlike the ongoing traditions of regional and (American) cultural geography, the humanist engagement took a distinctly philosophical turn looking (in what is now a familiar gesture) to continental European philosophy for inspiration. The philosophies of phenomenology and existentialism were central. It was in the mid-1970s that geographers began to seriously engage with philosophy – evoking the writing of Heidegger and Maurice Merleau-Ponty among others. As we shall see, it would be wrong to think of the focus on place as a return to the ideographic concerns with particular places that were central to human geography in the first half of the century. Rather place was seen as a universal and transhistorical part of the human condition. It was not so much places (in the world) that interested the humanists but "place" as an idea, concept, and way of being-in-the-world.

The two geographers who developed this new approach to place most thoroughly are Yi-Fu Tuan and Edward Relph. Yi-Fu Tuan's books *Topophilia* (1974b) and *Space and Place* (1977) have had an enormous impact on the history of human geography and, more specifically, the development of the idea of place. Tuan argued that, through human perception and experience, we get to know the world through places. The term "topophilia" was developed by Tuan to refer to the "affective bond between people and place" (Tuan 1974b, 4). This bond, this sense of attachment, is fundamental to the idea of place as a "field of care." Tuan defined place through a comparison with space. He develops a sense of space as an open arena of action and movement while place is about stopping and resting and becoming involved. While space is amenable to the abstraction of spatial science and economic rationality, place is amenable to discussions of things such as "value" and "belonging."

This kind of discussion of place is clearly much more than a discussion of location or region. Because place is a product of a "pause" and a chance of attachment it exists at many scales: "At one extreme a favorite armchair is a place, at the other extreme the whole earth" (Tuan 1977, 149).

> Place can be as small as the corner of a room or as large as the earth itself: that the earth is our place in the universe is a simple fact of observation to homesick astronauts... It is obvious that most definitions of place are quite arbitrary. Geographers tend to think of place as having the size of a settlement: the plaza within it may be counted a place, but usually not the individual houses, and certainly not that old rocking chair by the fireplace. (Tuan 1974a, 245)

Writing in 1974 (before humanistic geography was well known) it is obvious that Tuan was struggling with the abstractions of spatial science. "Unlike the spatial analyst, who must begin by making simplifying assumptions concerning man, the humanist begins with a deep commitment to the understanding of human nature in all its intricacy" (Tuan 1974a, 246). Spatial science simply missed out too much of the richness of human experience for Tuan and despite the lip service paid to "place" in definitions of geography, no one was really bothering to figure out what it was. It could not be measured or mapped and laws could not be deduced about or from it.

Edward Relph's approach to place was more explicit in its philosophical commitments to phenomenology. In *Place and Placelessness* Relph builds on what he describes as our practical knowledge of places – the very everyday and mundane fact of our knowing where to enact out lives (Relph 1976). We live in one place, work in another, play football in another. But we are also willing to protect our place against those who do not belong and we are frequently nostalgic for places we have left. These human responses, for Relph, reveal the deeper significance of place to human "being."

As with Tuan, Relph utilizes the comparison of place with space to make an argument for the significance of place to human life:

> Space is amorphous and intangible and not an entity that can be directly described and analysed. Yet, however we feel or explain space, there is nearly always some associated sense or concept of place. In general it seems that space provides the context for places but derives its meaning from particular places. (Relph 1976, 8)

The continuum which has place at one end and space at the other is simultaneously a continuum linking experience to abstraction. Places are experienced (Tuan's *Space and Place* is subtitled *The Perspective of Experience*).

Relph explicitly builds on the philosophy of Martin Heidegger and particularly the notions of *Dasein* and dwelling. For Heidegger, you will recall, *Dasein* was the very essence of existence – describing the way humans (and everything else) exist in-the-world. Seen in this way, place is a spiritual and philosophical endeavor that unites the natural and human worlds. A properly authentic existence to Heidegger is one rooted in place. If place is approached through the concepts of *Dasein* and dwelling, then to think of places as simply points on a map or even as "Toronto" or "Bombay" is a very shallow conception of place indeed. Note, though, how Heidegger chooses as his example a farmhouse in a forest. It is relatively straightforward to portray such a place as rooted as if in the soil. How this might apply to a modern place in an urban environment is a little harder to imagine. Heidegger's vision is romantic and nostalgic.

By developing the ideas of Heidegger, Relph sought to escape from simplistic notions of place as location. Relph quoted the philosopher Susanne Langer (also a favorite of Tuan's), noting that place, in the deeper sense, need not have any fixed location at all.

> A ship constantly changing its location is nonetheless a self-contained place, and so is a gypsy camp, an Indian camp, or a circus camp, however often it shifts its geodetic bearings. Literally we say a camp is in a place, but culturally it is a place. A gypsy camp is a different place from an Indian camp though it may be geographically where the Indian camp used to be. (Susanne Langer 1953 quoted in Relph 1976, 29)

Location, then, is not a necessary or sufficient condition of place. Relph works through a list of characteristics of place including their visuality (places have landscapes – we can see them), the sense of community that place supposedly engenders, the sense of time involved in establishing attachment to place and the value of "rootedness." But none of these, he argues, are enough to explain the deeper importance of place to human existence and experience. To get at this Relph returns to phenomenology.

The philosophy of phenomenology was developed by Franz Brentano and Edmund Husserl in the nineteenth century and its central concern is with what philosophers call "intentionality." The word intentionality refers to the "aboutness" of human consciousness. That is to say we cannot (the phenomenologist would argue) be conscious without being conscious of something. Consciousness constructs a relation between the self and the world. Relph's argument is that consciousness is not just of something – but something in its place. The only way humans can be humans is to be "in place." Place determines our experience.

> The basic meaning of place, its essence, does not therefore come from locations, nor from the trivial functions that places serve, nor from the community that occupies it, nor from superficial or mundane experiences…The essence of place lies in the largely unselfconscious intentionality that defines places as profound centers of human existence. (Relph 1976, 43)

Essence is a key word here. Phenomenologists saw as one of their principal tasks the discovery of essences. An essence is what makes something what it is. So rather than asking what this place or that place is like, the phenomenological approach to place asks what makes a place a place? What is it that the corner of a child's room shares with an urban garden or Kosovo? Clearly this is not an interest in the particular but a rather grand investigation of a central component of the human world.

At heart, this phenomenological enterprise involved the acknowledgment that to be human is to be "in place." To the humanist, ontological priority was given to the human immersion in place rather than the abstractions of geometric space. As Casey has put it "To live is to live locally, and know is first of all to know the place one is in" (Casey 1996, 18). This phenomenological focus on place as experience echoes an earlier observation by Lukerman.

> The study of place is the subject matter of geography because consciousness of place is an immediately apparent part of reality, not a sophisticated thesis; knowledge of place is a simple fact of experience. (Lukerman 1964, 168)

Place is therefore a pre-scientific fact of life – based on the way we experience the world.

The humanistic strand in human geography is a continuous one that informs contemporary debate in many ways. Robert Sack has written of the connections between place and morality, arguing that in the (post)modern world the primary form our relationship to place takes is often one of consumption (Sack 1992). We are sold products in consumption places and they are advertised with reference to a variety of fantastic contexts. The net result of all of this, he argues, is a diminished sense of the consequences of our actions. Morality, to Sack, is based on a knowledge of the consequences of what we do. Consumption, through the disguise of production processes, hides the consequences of our purchase and thus creates an amoral consumer's world. A key part of this equation is the spatial scope of such consequences. Hypermodernity is characterized by a characteristic globalism that makes each local action potentially global in its consequences. It's all too much for the individual to process. In the background to Sack's consumer's world lies the alternative of place-based actions where morality is possible due to the close proximity and accountability of the producers of goods. Note how this story of place insinuates the dangerous character of flows and dynamism which disconnect people from place boundedness. This theme, the threat of mobility, is one we shall return to later.

Place as Home?

For many, the most familiar example of place and its significance to people is the idea of home. It is the first example of place in this book. For Tuan, geography is the study of Earth as the home of people (Tuan 1991). By transforming the Earth into home we create places at myriad different levels. Tuan argues that the making of places at all scales is seen as the production of a certain kind of homeliness. Home is an exemplary kind of place where people feel a sense of attachment and rootedness. Home, more than anywhere else, is seen as a center of meaning and a field of care. David Seamon has also argued that home is an intimate place of rest where a person can withdraw from the hustle of the world outside and have some degree of control over what happens within a limited space (Seamon 1979). Home is where you can be yourself. In this sense home acts as a kind of metaphor for place in general.

The centrality of home to humanistic approaches to place owes much both to Heidegger's focus on dwelling as the ideal kind of authentic existence and to the work of Bachelard (1994). In *The Poetics of Space*, you will recall, Bachelard considers the house/home as a primal space that acts as a first world or first universe that then frames our understandings of all the spaces outside. The home is an intimate space where experience is particularly intense. To Bachelard, the interior arrangement of the house constitutes not one homogeneous place but rather a series of places with their own memories, imaginings, and dreams. Thus Bachelard distinguishes between the attic and the basement where the attic is a place of the intellect and rationality and the basement is the place of the unconscious and of nightmares – "The unconscious cannot be civilized. It takes a candle when it goes to the cellar" (Bachelard 1994, 19). To Bachelard, then, the house/ home is a particularly privileged kind of place that frames the way people go on to think about the wider universe.

This idea of home as a fundamental place has been questioned by feminists. The feminist geographer Gillian Rose has considered the role of home as place in geography. In her account of humanistic geography (a chapter titled "No place for women") Rose finds much to applaud in the efforts of Tuan, Relph, and others. Their willingness to introduce issues of home and the body, for instance, share much with the concerns of feminist geographers. What she finds troubling, however, is the way the idea of place as home is discussed in humanistic geography.

> Although it was often noted that home need not necessarily be a family house, images of the domestic recur in their work as universal, even biological, experiences. Tuan remarked that "human identification with the familiar, nurturing place has a biological basis." This enthusiasm for home and for what is associated with the domestic, in the context of the erasure of women from humanistic studies, suggests to me that humanistic geographers are working with a masculinist notion of home/place. (Rose 1993, 53)

Rose points out that many women do not share the rosy of view of home/ place that humanistic geographers place at the center of the discipline. Communities can be stifling and homes can be and often are places of drudgery, abuse, and neglect. Many women, Rose argues, would not recognize a view of home/place that is "conflict-free, caring, nurturing and almost mystically venerated by the humanists" ((Rose 1993, 56).

> So, to white feminists who argue that the home was "the central site of the oppression of women," there seemed little reason to celebrate a sense of belonging to the home, and even less, I would add, to support the humanistic geographers' claim that home provides the ultimate sense of place. (Rose 1993, 55)

While humanists claim that place is a universal experience (while at the same time using the word "man" as the universal person) they fail to recognize the differences between people and their relation to place. In the search for "essence" – "difference" has no place.

Not all feminists share Rose's view although most would share her suspicion of the idea of home as always warm and caring. The black feminist author bell hooks has written of home as a place of resistance (hooks 1990). As a black child growing up in a starkly segregated society, hooks experienced her home as a place of care and relative freedom from the oppression black people suffered in the world outside and, especially, in the homes of white people where they worked as domestic servants. To hooks, home and the activities that go into making home can have significance as forms of resistance in an oppressive white world. Home may indeed act as a particular kind of safe place where (some) people are relatively free to forge their own identities. For hooks, homeplace is an empowering place.

Radical Human Geography and the Politics of Place

Discussions of place as home begin to reveal some of the political issues that surround place. While the geographical engagement with phenomenological enquiry rescued the notion of place from oblivion it simultaneously constructed a notion of place which some see as essentialist and exclusionary, based on notions of rooted authenticity that are increasingly unsustainable in the (post)modern world. Heidegger, Vidal, and Sauer, tended to focus on rural images and places in order to make their arguments about regions and place. At the beginning of the twenty-first century it is very hard to see how these observations can be applied even to modern rurality, let alone the modern metropolis. This has led geographers informed by Marxism, feminism, and poststructuralism to shy away from place as a concept. When they have engaged with place it has been in a critical mode – pointing out how places are socially constructed and how these constructions are founded on acts of exclusion.

The Marxist geographer David Harvey, for instance, has argued that the significance of place has increased under the conditions of flexible accumulation, postmodernity, and time–space compression (Harvey 1996). He suggests this because, as he sees it, places are under all kinds of threats from variously: the restructuring of economic spatial relations at a global level, the increased mobility of production, capital, merchanting and marketing, and the increasing need to differentiate between places in order to compete. Place, in Harvey's lexicon, is a form of fixed capital which exists in tension with other forms of mobile capital. The tension between the fixed and the mobile produces cycles of place investment and disinvestment which contribute to an unstable process of uneven development across the globe. In the story that Harvey tells, place has a more ambivalent role than in the celebrations of humanism. Place is certainly threatened by the hypermobility of flexible capital, mass communications, and transportation. Political struggles over place, therefore, often provide opportunities for resistance to the mobile forces of capitalism. But struggles for place identity also appeal to the parochial and exclusive forces of bigotry and nationalism. The identification of place usually involves an us/them distinction in which the other is devalued (see Chapter 4 for an extended discussion of this theme).

Around the late 1980s geographers began to seriously engage with the wider fields of social theory and cultural studies. The distinction between so-called humanistic geographers on the one hand and radical geographers on the other began to break down and a new cultural geography informed by Raymond Williams, Antonio Gramsci, and the work of the Birmingham School of Cultural Studies emerged. On both sides of the Atlantic geographers began to confidently assert the importance of geography to critical theory. Class, gender, and race have so often been treated as if they happened on the head of a pin. Well they don't – they happen in space and place. By taking space and place seriously, it was argued, we can provide another tool to demystify and understand the forces that affect and manipulate our everyday lives.

It was in this context that I wrote *In Place/Out of Place* (Cresswell 1996). In this book I argued that people, things, and practices were often strongly linked to particular places and that when this link was broken – when people acted "out of place" – they were deemed to have committed a "transgression." I used the examples of graffiti artists in New York City, the peace campers of Greenham Common (UK) and New Age travelers in the British countryside. In each case people and practices were considered (by the media, government, etc.) to have transgressed the supposedly common-sense link between place and the things that go on it. The purpose of this work was to show how place does not have meanings that are natural and obvious but ones that are created by some people with more power than others to define what is and is not appropriate. It also showed how people are able to resist the construction of expectations about practice through place by using places and their established meanings in subversive ways. Throughout, issues of age, gender, class, lifestyle, sexuality, and ethnicity were at the fore. All of these had been largely ignored by traditions such as regional geography and humanistic geography. We will return to these themes of exclusion and transgression in Chapter 6.

Critical cultural geographers began to use place in myriad ways which revealed the complicated connections between place, meaning, and power.

Benjamin Forest, for instance, considered how the gay population of West Hollywood in California successfully mobilized symbols of gay identity such as creativity and progressive politics during the campaign to incorporate West Hollywood in 1984 (Forest 1995). He argued that having a politically constituted place as a geographical focus of gay identity allowed the gay community to construct an identity based on more than sexual acts. Through attachment of place, Forest argued, gay identity could be seen as a kind of ethnicity rather than as a sickness or perversion. In other words place acted to normalize and naturalize the identity of gay people.

Figure 2.1 Gay liberation monument, Christopher Park, New York City. A positive form of identity construction through place. Source: photo by Dennis (DennisInAmsterdam on flickr.com) (http://flickr.com/photos/rith/298094205/) [CC-BY-SA-2.0 (http://creativecommons.org/licenses/by-sa/2.0)], via Wikimedia Commons.

Figure 2.2   The Millennium Gate at Chinatown, Vancouver, Canada. A generic symbol of Chinese identity? Source: photo by MRDXII (Own work) [CC-BY-SA-3.0 (http://creativecommons.org/licenses/by-sa/3.0)], via Wikimedia Commons.

Another example of the critical cultural approach to the production of places is Kay Anderson's examination of the construction of Chinatown in Vancouver, Canada (Anderson 1991). Anderson asks how it is that a place known as Chinatown has come to exist in major cities across the world. Many people, she argues, see the existence of Chinatown as evidence of a naturalized connection between Chinese culture and the places that Chinese people settle in around the world. In other words Chinese people arrive and they construct a place full of Chinese restaurants, grocery stores, and pagodas. Anderson's argument is that these places cannot simply be read as symbols of essential Chineseness but rather that such places are ideologically constructed as places of difference. In the case of Vancouver she traces the arrival of the Chinese in the west of Canada in response to the discovery of gold and their subsequent work on the railroads and in stores and laundries. Over time they were subjected to a set of discourses among white people about the supposed "nature" of the Chinese as irredeemably different and inferior. Gradually, Chinese immigrants began to settle in one area of Vancouver and this clustering alarmed white onlookers. White elites portrayed the Chinese as a form of pollution and disease that threatened white racial purity. By the late 1880s people began to use the word "Chinatown," a term imported from San Francisco.

> Well before any substantial settlement of Chinese was identified as such in Vancouver, a "place" for them already had a distinct reality in local vocabulary and culture. "Had Dante been able to visit Chinatown, San Francisco," said Secretary of State J. Chapleau in 1885, "he would have added yet darker strokes of horror to his inferno." (Anderson 1996, 219)

As Chinese people began to gather around Dupont Street this new "Chinatown" began to be seen as a natural center of vice and depravity, full of dirt, disease and moral failure (opium dens, gambling, and prostitution). The racial designation "Chinese" was seen as synonymous with moral failure and a particular place – Chinatown. For many years the place was put alongside water, sewage, and infectious diseases under the responsibility of the municipal sanitary officer.

Anderson shows how "Chinatown" was not simply a natural reflection of Chinese culture but the result of negotiation with those with the power to define place (the media, government, etc.). More recently this socially constructed place has become a tourist attraction where white tourists can visit the "exotic other" and enjoy the old ideas and vice and depravity in a sanitized form. Despite the fact that the place is now seen as safe and even attractive, it is still serves to reaffirm a moral order of "them" and "us."

Forest's paper on West Hollywood and Anderson's consideration of Chinatown feature the idea of place at the heart of their analyses. They are not simply papers about particular places – though we do learn about Vancouver and West Hollywood by reading them – but they are about the way place works in a world of social hierarchies. In the case of West Hollywood, place plays a positive role of affirming gay identity through its inscription in place. Here the linking of place and identity is a political choice of self-affirmation. In the case of Chinatown, place plays a negative role of naturalizing white Western views of Chinese immorality and inferiority by attaching a particular white view of Chinese culture to a place known as Chinatown.

Place for critical cultural geographers from the late 1980s onwards was a concept that needed to be understood through the lens of social and cultural conflict. Issues of race, class, gender, sexuality, and a host of other social relations were at the center of this analysis. Place was not simply an outcome of social processes though; it was, once established, a tool in the creation, maintenance, and transformation of relations of domination, oppression, and exploitation. By fixing Chinese identity in place, the cultural and social elites of Vancouver were able to more easily cast Chinese culture and the Chinese themselves in a negative light. By successfully lobbying for the incorporation of West Hollywood, gay people were able to produce an affirmative vision of their own lifestyle.

Place as "Being-in-the-World" versus Place as Social Construct

The geographer Robert Sack, and the philosophers of place Edward Casey and J. E. Malpas, sought to reinstate a much more fundamental role for place in social life. Their approach can best be explained by contrasting it to the following claim by David Harvey:

> Place, in whatever guise, is like space and time, a social construct. This is the baseline proposition from which I start. The only interesting question that can then be asked is: by what social process(es) is place constructed? (Harvey 1996, 261)

The assertion of the importance of talking of places as socially constructed nicely outlines the dominant approach to matters of place in contemporary critical human geography. To say a place is socially constructed is to say that it is not natural, and given that human forces made a place, then human forces equally importantly can undo it. This approach is favored by those with a progressive political agenda as it indicates that if things are one way now, they might be entirely different later. It is the approach taken by the critical human geographers in the previous section. To say something is socially constructed is to say that it is within human power to change it. So what is it that is socially constructed about place? Two things stand out: meaning and materiality.

If we say that New York's Lower East Side is a social construct we are saying that the way we experience that place, the meanings we ascribe to it, come out of a social milieu dominated by Western cultural values and the forces of capitalism. They are also produced by the media, by politicians, and by the people who live there. We might have read in the paper about riots in Tompkins Square Park and be (unreasonably) afraid to go there. We might see the graffiti, murals, cafés, and shops and think it's an invigorating and diverse place to be. Whatever meaning it appears to have there is little doubt that it comes from "society."

To say a place is socially constructed is also to say that the materiality – the very fabric of a place – is a product of society too. The buildings, the parks, the trees that have been planted, the roads and restaurants have literally been built – often for the production of profit but also for a range of other reasons. The community gardens are not "natural" but have been put there by the tireless efforts of local residents. It is hard to believe that anyone, in a place like the Lower East Side, could think of the place as anything other than a social construct.

In many ways these points seem obvious and we may wonder why Harvey bothers making them at all. But there is another profound way of thinking about place that sees it as something much deeper than a social construct, as something irreducible and essential to being human.

Sack, in *Homo Geographicus*, makes the following claim:

> Indeed, privileging the social in modern geography, and especially in the reductionist sense that "everything is socially constructed," does as much disservice to geographical analysis as a whole as has privileging the natural in the days of environmental determinism, or concentrating only on the mental or intellectual in some areas of humanistic geography. While one or other may be more important for a particular situation at a particular time, none is determinate of the geographical. (Sack 1997, 2)

Sack clearly thinks that Harvey is wrong when he asserts that "the only interesting question that can then be asked is: by what social process(es) is place constructed?" To Sack, place's role in the human world runs a lot deeper than that – it is a force that cannot be reduced to the social, the natural, or the cultural. It is, rather, a phenomenon that brings these worlds together and, indeed, in part produced them.

Sack is not the only one to make this point. Contemporary philosophy has also seen a mini renaissance of interest in the concept of place. In recent years two philosophers stand out for their detailed examinations of the idea of place. Not only do they provide detailed accounts of the role of place in philosophers such as Heidegger (to which I am indebted) but they make their own cases for the primacy of place in our understanding of the world.

These are Edward Casey and J. E. Malpas. To a philosopher such as Malpas, geographers and others (despite a 2000-plus-year history of thinking about place) have failed to really attend to the complexity of place (or, indeed, space) as a concept. Philosophers think differently and it is a special kind of attentiveness to concepts that philosophers bring to the interdisciplinary table. Place, Malpas argues, "often appears either as a subjective overlay on the reality of materialized spatiality (place is space plus human value or "meaning"...) or else as merely an arbitrary designated position within a spatial field" (Malpas n.d.). Malpas wants there to be more to the concept of place than these commonly used definitions. So what does he want to add? He argues for thinking about place as both internally heterogeneous as well as different from other places beyond it. Places are, in other words, relational both inside and out. "No place exists except in relation to other places, and every place contains other places that are related within it" (Malpas n.d.). Places also carry space within them in Malpas's terms. Places are internally open – they have room within them – but room that occurs within a boundary. Places in Malpas's "philosophical topography" are bounded yet open, temporally dynamic, surface oriented and relational. More importantly still, and following Heidegger, "place is central to understanding human being, and in fact, to understanding... any sort of coming to appearance at all" (Malpas n.d.). Malpas clearly sits in the tradition of Plato, Aristotle, Heidegger, and others who see place as much more than a segment of the inhabited earth – even a meaningful one. Rather they see it as a primary basis for existence – for "coming to appearance." This is very different from the currently hegemonic position taken up by geographers and others that places are primarily socially constructed.

Consider the words of Malpas:

> The idea of place encompasses both the idea of the social activities and institutions that are expressed in and through the structure of a particular place (and which can be seen as partially determinative of that place) and the idea of the physical objects and events in the world (along with the associated causal processes) that constrain, and are sometimes constrained by, those social activities and institutions. There is no doubt that the ordering of a particular place – and the specific way in which a society orders space and time – is not independent of social ordering (inasmuch as it encompasses the social, so place is partially elaborated by means of the social, just as place is also elaborated in relation to orderings deriving from individual subjects and from underlying physical structures). However this does not legitimate the claim that place, space or time are merely social constructions.

Indeed the social does not exist prior to place nor is it given expression except in and through place – and through spatialised, temporalised ordering... It is within the structure of place that the very possibility of the social arises. (Malpas 1999, 35–36)

Once place is said to be a social construct then place itself becomes relatively neglected. Malpas makes his argument in the following way.

Moreover, the mere fact of variability in some phenomenon does not imply that there is nothing that can be said about the phenomenon beyond its particular instantiations nor does it imply that the phenomenon is wholly derivative of the other factors that determine it. The fact that practices surrounding death and dying, for example, vary enormously from one society to another does not imply that those practices cannot be conceptualized in a more generalized way that, while it may draw upon specific instances, nevertheless goes beyond any particular such instance. Thus we can talk about the human experience of death and dying, and the practices that surround it, even while acknowledging the variability of those practices. In fact, being able to go beyond any particular instance of some phenomenon is precisely what is involved in having a concept that applies to that phenomenon. (Malpas n.d.)

Place (and space), Malpas argues, have to be conceptualized on their own terms and not seen as simply remnants of more fundamental social forces. Indeed, it may even be the case that place must come first – that the possibility of society – and thus of social construction – only exists because of place.

Note that Malpas, and Sack for that matter, do not deny that specific places are the products of society and culture. They insist, however, that place, in a general sense, adds up to a lot more than that. They point out that society itself is inconceivable without place – that the social (and the cultural) is geographically constructed. On the face of it this does not seem a lot different from the claim that the social and the spatial are "mutually constitutive" – a claim which is central to some forms of social constructionism. But the claims of Sack and Malpas are different from that due to their claim that the realm of the "social" has no particular privilege in discussions of place. Malpas looks once more to Heidegger's philosophy of place in which human beings are characterized in terms of their "being in the world." This relation between humans and place, Malpas argues, is not like apples being in a box but a sense of necessary relation – it is how we are.

Place is instead that within and with respect to which subjectivity is itself established – place is not founded on subjectivity, but is rather that on which subjectivity is founded. Thus one does not first have a subject that apprehends certain features of the world in terms of the idea of place; instead, the structure of subjectivity is given in and through the structure of place. (Malpas 1999, 35)

This is quite different from the claims of the social constructionists that humans construct both the meaning of place and the material structure of places. Malpas and Sack are arguing that humans cannot construct anything without being first in place – that place is primary to the construction of meaning and society. Place is primary because it is the experiential fact of our existence. Again, this is not new – it reflects both Heidegger's insistence on the necessary relation between things and places and the much older Aristotelian notion of Albertus Magnus that things belong somewhere.

The problem for students of place with this view of the world is that it is rather short on empirical detail. If you read the work of Sack, Malpas, and Casey you will find few extended accounts of particular places. Because they are talking about place in general it is hard to use specific examples to make the case. Indeed, like Heidegger and his Black Forest cabin, they tend to use imagined and idealized examples or "thought experiments." So what might such a view tell us if we returned to New York's Lower East Side?

First of all, it clearly would not tell us much about the processes that went into making the place what it is. It would have more or less nothing to say about the processes of gentrification or the construction of parks in urban areas or the presence of Puerto Rican restaurants. It would not be able to explain the social unrest that has periodically rocked the area. These are all the kinds of things that a Marxist geographer like David Harvey seeks to explain by his insistence that places are socially constructed. But are these, as he claims, the only interesting questions? The place-centered approach of Sack, Malpas, and others would suggest that what is going on in the Lower East Side, or anywhere else for that matter, is simply an example of what is going on in all human life: a struggle over the very basis of human experience – the need for place as a bedrock of human meaning and social relations.

These complicated arguments are important and necessary for a thorough understanding of the idea of place as it is used in geography and elsewhere in the social sciences and humanities as well as in creative arts. Perhaps it helps to reconsider the notion of social construction. All kinds of things are socially constructed – ideas about space and time, particle physics, brain surgery, toothpaste, nuclear bombs, television, and fashion are all, with different degrees of obviousness, constructed within particular societies with particular, usually hierarchical, social relations. Some things are equally clearly (at least to this author) not social constructions – gravity, the planet Earth, life and death, glacial moraines. All of these things have socially constructed meanings without which it is impossible to talk about them but the things themselves are there whether we construct them or not. So what kind of thing is place? Place, some would argue, is neither like toothpaste (which once did not exist and in the future will be redundant), nor gravity (which exists completely free of human will or consciousness). It is a construction of humanity but a necessary one – one that human life is impossible to conceive of without. In other words there was no "place" before there was humanity but once we came into existence then place did too. A future without place is simply inconceivable (unlike a future without toothpaste). Although the social construction of place is not the main theme of Sack and Malpas, their arguments suggest that place is a kind of "necessary social construction" – something we have to construct in order to be human. This is not to say that we have to construct the Lower East Side, Kosovo, or London's Millennium Dome in all their particularity but that in their absence places would still exist – just different ones.

Assembling Place

Think back to the account of place in regional geography. Recall how Richard Hartshorne, like many other geographers at the time, insisted on the exceptional status of geography as a science of the particular – a discipline that focused on the particular way in which things combined to make a region. Geography was seen as the study of "the total combination of phenomena in each place, different from those in every other place" (Hartshorne 1939, 462). While Hartshorne stood out for his desire to provide a philosophical basis for regional geography, other geographers made essentially the same claim – "that which geography, in exchange for the help it has received from other sciences, can bring to the common treasury, is the capacity not to break apart what nature has assembled" (Martin *et al.* 1993, 193). One reading of such statements is to see them as quaintly old-fashioned – a relic of a bygone age which lacked sophistication. Another reading, however, and one I prefer, sees these as early statements of a view of the world that is now referred to as assemblage theory. It also foreshadows a phenomenological emphasis on place as a site of gathering which occurs in the work of Heidegger and, more recently in Casey. Let's take the latter first.

> Places gather: this I take to be the second essential trait (i.e. beyond the role of the lived body) revealed by a phenomenological topo-analysis. Minimally, places gather things in their midst – where "things" connote various animate and inanimate entities. Places also gather experiences and histories, even languages and thoughts. Think only of what it means to go back to a place you know, finding it full of memories and expectations, old things and new things, the familiar and strange, and much more besides. What else is capable of this massively diversified holding action?…The power belongs to place itself, and it is a power of gathering. (Casey 1996, 24)

This emphasis on gathering mirrors the foci of Hartshorne and others and presents it in a new philosophical language. The process of gathering (things, emotions, people, memories, etc.) suggests that there is a relationship between the inside of a place (which gathers) and an outside (from where things are gathered). It underlines the relational nature of place – the necessity of a place being related to its outside. It therefore suggests a relation between place and things on the move – a theme we will develop in the next chapter.

Assemblage theory is a more recent, poststructuralist, take on this act of gathering and combination. It derives from the work of the French philosophers Gilles Deleuze and Félix Guattari and has been fully developed by the philosopher Manuel DeLanda in his book *A New Philosophy of Society* (DeLanda 2006, Deleuze and Guattari 1987). Assemblage theory has become influential across disciplines, including in geography and architecture (Dovey 2010, Anderson and McFarlane 2011). An assemblage is a unique whole "whose properties emerge from the interactions between parts" (DeLanda 2006, 5). Assemblages are distinct from organic structures which are also assembled from parts but depend on each part in order to exist. In an organic structure, if you take away a constituent part, the structure would cease to exist in a recognizable way. With an assemblage, constituent parts can be removed and replaced. The parts can then enter other assemblages and contribute to new "unique wholes." The ways in which parts are combined in an assemblage are not structurally necessary or pre-ordained. They are not directed by some higher force. Their combination is contingent.

Places are ideal candidates for the status of assemblages. Indeed, De-Landa's book proceeds through a series of scales of place (neighborhood, city, nation, etc.) to make its argument. The architectural theorist, Kim Dovey, illustrates this nicely.

> For instance, a street is not a thing nor is it just a collection of discrete things. The buildings, trees, cars, sidewalks, goods, people, signs, etc. all come together to become a street, but it is the connections between them that makes it an assemblage or a place. It is the relations of buildings–sidewalk–roadway; the flows of traffic, people and goods; the interconnections of public to private space, and of this street to the city, that makes it a "street" and distinguish it from other place assemblages such as parks, plazas, free-ways, shopping malls and marketplaces. Within this assemblage the sidewalk is nothing more than a further assemblage of connections between things and practices. The assemblage is also dynamic – trees and people grow and die, buildings are constructed and demolished. It is the flows of life, traffic, goods and money that give the street its intensity and its sense of place. All places are assemblages. (Dovey 2010, 16)

You can think of your home in this way. The place where you live is clearly a particular place. It is also a gathering of things, memories, stories, and practices. It includes doors and windows, floors and ceilings. It also includes appliances, photos, bookshelves, the food in the fridge and the notes on the door. All of these things make it a unique place – a unique assemblage. And yet it is different every day. The food gets eaten and replaced. The notes on the fridge door change. Even the wood that forms the floors, doors, and window frames is slowly eroding. Occasionally it is replaced. It is also the case that many of the parts that make up your home could be removed and used in another home. Things such as doors and fridges tend to be mass-produced. But still it is the assemblage that is your place – your home. It is a discrete thing that is made up from the relation between parts that are always changing. All places can be thought of in this way.

Assemblage theory, as developed by DeLanda, is more precise than simply the observation that some things are made from contingent con-nections between parts. DeLanda also describes two key axes that make up an assemblage. One axis connects the two key roles played by elements of an assemblage – expressive roles and material roles. Once again these are easily mapped on to the ways we things about place as having a material existence (locale, landscape) and an expressive existence (in so far as places are meaningful, cultural entities). The second axis links forces that make a place cohere (territorializing forces) and those that pull it apart (deterritorializing forces).

> the former are referred to as processes of territorialization and the latter as processes of deterritorialization. One and the same assemblage can have components working to stabilize its identity as well as components forcing it to change or even transforming it into a different assemblage. In fact, one and the same component may participate in both processes by exercising different sets of capacities. (DeLanda 2006, 12)

Returning to the place you call home, you can see that there are forces at work that stabilize its identity, ranging from the legal structures that make it your house to the physical forces that hold the walls, floors, and ceilings together. You can also think of processes that might make it less stable – the natural forces of entropy or the lines that lead out from the home to the wider world.

If we think of the early statements of regional geography, the phenomenological emphasis on gathering, and the poststructuralist notion of assemblage we can see how places are syncretic wholes made up of parts and how any particular place is connected to the wide world beyond from which things are gathered and to which things are dispersed. Any consideration of the unique collection of parts that makes up a place has to take into account the relations between that place and what lies beyond it. This is a central theme in the following chapter.

Conclusions: Versions of Place

In this chapter we have explored the changing conceptions of place in philosophy, human geography, and beyond. We have seen how place was at the center of the philosophies of Plato and Aristotle and how Heidegger and Bachelard made place key to their phenomenological investigations. Place, in a common-sense way, has always been central to the discipline of geography but relatively undeveloped as an idea until the 1970s and the emergence of humanistic geography founded on phenomenology. Writers such as Tuan and Relph, and later Sack, Casey, and Malpas, developed the idea of place as a central meaningful component in human life – a center of meaning and field of care that formed the basis for human interaction. Critical human geographers, informed by Marxism, feminism, and cultural studies, were keen to show how places were socially constructed in contexts of unequal power relations and how they represented relations of domination and exploitation. Most recently there has been return to thinking about place as a combination of parts that links the inside of a place to what lies beyond – places as syncretic sites of gathering and assemblage.

Place is clearly a complicated concept. It is all the more confusing because, at first glance, it appears to be obvious and common-sense. It is worth thinking back over the various approaches to place in this chapter to consider the different ways that different writers have written about place. In many ways they appear to be writing about quite separate things. Regional geographers talk about places as discrete areas of land with their own ways of life. Humanists and philosophers write of place as a fundamental way of being in the world. Radical geographers investigate the way places are constructed as reflections of power. Is it possible that they all hold nuggets of value for contemporary theorists of place? Or do they cancel each other out? Is there one "place" at the center of the debate?

The central argument about place in geography and beyond seems to be between those who write of place in terms of individual places – their locations, their boundaries, and their associated meanings and practices (regional geographers, specific accounts of the politics of particular places, etc.) – and those who want to argue for a deeper primal sense of place (humanistic geographers, philosophers of place). Maybe both exist. The kinds of places we inhabit – favorite rooms, neighborhoods, nations – are all indeed analyzable as social products – as political outcomes and tools in the ongoing struggles between sectors of society. And, indeed, they are all describable in the way regional geographers have described them in the past. But perhaps these places are all instances or examples of a deeper sense that humanity has to exist in place. It would be wrong to romanticize this sense of place as always rosy and "homelike" (in the idealized sense of home). Some places are evil, oppressive, and exploitative. But they are still the way we experience the world – through and in place. And perhaps it is because place is so primal to human existence that it becomes such a powerful political force in its socially constructed forms. It is impossible, after all, to think of a world without place.

Through the history of the idea of place it is possible to see (at least) three levels at which place is approached.

1   A descriptive approach to place. This approach most closely resembles the common-sense idea of the world being a set of places, each of which can be studied as a unique and particular entity. This ideographic approach to place was the one taken by regional geographers but continues to the present day. The concern here is with the distinctiveness and particularity of places. A writer taking this approach might want to research and write about "The geography of the North of England" or "The soul of San Francisco."

2   A social constructionist approach to place. This approach is still interested in the particularity of places but only as instances of more general underlying social processes. Marxists, feminists, and poststructuralists might take this approach to place. Looking at the social construction of place involves explaining the unique attributes of a place (say the Docklands of London or the Baltimore harbor) by showing how these places are instances of wider processes of the construction of place in general under conditions of capitalism, patriarchy, heterosexism, post-colonialism, and a host of other structural conditions.

3   A phenomenological approach of place. This approach is not particularly interested in the unique attributes of particular places nor is it primarily concerned with the kinds of social forces that are involved in the construction of particular places. Rather it seeks to define the essence of human existence as one that is necessarily and importantly "in-place." This approach is less concerned with "places" and more interested in "Place." Humanistic geographers, neo-humanists and phenomenological philosophers all take this approach to place.

These three levels should not be seen as discrete sets as there is clearly some overlap between them. Broadly speaking they represent three levels of "depth" in approaches to place with level 1 representing a concern with the surface of the world as we see it and level 3 representing a deep universal sense of what place means to humanity. It would be wrong however to think that these correspond in some easy way to "importance." Research at all three levels (and the ones in between) is important and necessary to understand the full complexity of the role of place in human life.

Recently, geographers and others have attempted to write accounts of place that have some of the syncretic and descriptive characteristics of early regional geographies but are informed by phenomenology, poststructuralism, and assemblage theory (among other approaches). They are also marked by an increased willingness to engage in creative writing practices.

These represent a practice of "place-writing" that attempts to grapple with particular places in all their complexity. These writers take a place, usually quite small in scale, and use a number of creative strategies to present the place to the reader as an entanglement of diverse elements and strands using stories of people and things to recreate what Doreen Massey has called the "throwntogetherness" of place (Massey 2005). These long essays on individual places thus resemble the regional geography tradition of the first half of the twentieth century but are more likely to be concerned with the ways in which a place is constructed in relation to what lies beyond it (Price 2004, Ogden 2011).

An excellent example of this re-invigorated place-writing is Patricia Price's *Dry Place*. This book focuses on the area around the Mexico–US border and does so by approaching the place through a number of different narratives, or stories, about the place. Price does not claim to be describing, in great detail, a place that exists out there, just waiting to found and described. Rather she insists on the power of narratives, often competing narratives, in bringing a place into being through story-telling:

> narratives about people's places in places continuously materialize the entity we call place. In its materializations, however, there are conflicts, silences, exclusions. Tales are retold and their meanings wobble and shift over time. Multiple claims are made. Some stories are deemed heretical. The resulting dislocations, discontinuities, and disjunctures work to continually destabilize that which appears to be stable: a unitary, univocal place. (Price 2004, 4)

Dry Place focuses on just this process of story-telling, counter-posing stories such as those accounts of manifest destiny told by the agents of Anglo-American expansionism with other, less dominant, stories that contest claims to the southwestern landscape. The writing strategy in the book is also notable as it includes some of Price's own story-telling – through her own creative writing practice of poetry.

> This smooth space from which so much is conjured
> and into which so much has been distilled
> Embroidered by patient hands, surgical masks, blessed hearts, sacred feet
> Colored and flavored with blood, sweat, tears, hopes, dreams, fears
> Ground into dry sand
> Pulverized and dribbled
> A shaman's scribbles
> A Kool-Aid trail

Naxca lines in the shape of a snail
A chain of stores
A silver lining
Borderlining

(Price 2004, 174)

Another exemplary, poly-vocal, account of a place is the anthropologist Laura A. Ogden's account of the Florida Everglades, *Swamplife* (Ogden 2011). While Price focused on the gathering of narratives in place, Ogden's book traces the entanglement of alligators, people, mangroves, and their stories in a beautiful and fractured account of the Everglades as a place and landscape. The main chapters of the book are interspersed with the stories of the violent Ashley gang, a notorious group of outlaws whose stories permeate the Everglades. But these stories are not allowed to dominate the place in which "Animals and humans emerge as collaborative agents of territory within these refrains, with animals (particularly alligators) shaping the territorial practices of hunters and hunters shaping the territorial practices of alligators" (Ogden 2011, 32). *Swamplife* is an account of a place but it is a stylistically and theoretically innovative one that draws much from poststructuralism and assemblage theory. It does not attempt to give a complete picture of the place/region but instead revels in the indeterminacy of place.

Yet in the quest for revelation through breaking down, the joy in invention, experimentation, and play often gets lost. Instead of using ideas to break things down (reduction), I am interested in using ideas to build things up (production). What gets produced, in this book at least, are maps of the remembered landscape. But these maps are not cartographies of "the way it really was." On the contrary, these maps will only help us get a bit less lost (Ogden 2011, 26).

In the place-writing practices of Ogden and Price (amongst others), we see all of the three levels of place theory in action simultaneously. They are certainly descriptive accounts of individual places but they are also grappling with the phenomenological significance of place to its inhabitants (both human and non-human) and the ways in which power and society are producing, and being produced by, place.

References

Amin, A. (2004) Regions unbound: Towards a new politics of place. *Geografiska Annaler. Series B, Human Geography* 86, 33–44.

Anderson, B. and McFarlane, C. (2011) Assemblage and geography. *Area* 43, 124–127.

Anderson, K. (1991) *Vancouver's Chinatown: Racial Discourse in Canada, 1875–1980*. Montreal, McGill-Queen's University Press.

Anderson, K. (1996) Cultural hegemony and the race-definition process in Chinatown, Vancouver: 1880–1980, in *Social Geography: A Reader*, ed. C. Hamnett, London, Arnold, pp. 209–235.

Bachelard, G. (1994) *The Poetics of Space*. Boston, Beacon Press.

Buttimer, A. (1971) *Society and Milieu in the French Geographic Tradition*. Chicago, Rand McNally for the Association of American Geographers.

Buttimer, A. and Seamon, D. (1980) *The Human Experience of Space and Place*. New York, St. Martin's Press.

Casey, E. (1996) How to get from space to place in a fairly short stretch of time, in *Senses of Place*, ed. S. Feld and K. Baso, Santa Fe, School of American Research, pp. 14–51.

Casey, E. S. (1998) *The Fate of Place: A Philosophical History*. Berkeley, University of California Press.

Christaller, W. (1966 [1933]) *Central Places in Southern Germany*. New York, Prentice-Hall.

Cresswell, T. (1996) *In Place/Out of Place: Geography, Ideology and Transgression*. Minneapolis, University of Minnesota Press.

Cresswell, T. (2006) *On the Move: Mobility in the Modern Western World*. New York, Routledge.

Cresswell, T. (2013) *Geographic Thought: A Critical Introduction*. Oxford, Wiley-Blackwell.

DeLanda, M. (2006) *A New Philosophy of Society: Assemblage Theory and Social Complexity*. London and New York, Continuum.

Deleuze, G. and Guattari, F. (1987) *A Thousand Plateaus: Capitalism and Schizophrenia*. Minneapolis, University of Minnesota Press.

Dovey, K. (2010) *Becoming Places: Urbanism/Architecture/Identity/Power*. London, Routledge.

Entrikin, J. N. (1991) *The Betweenness of Place: Towards a Geography of Modernity*. Baltimore, Johns Hopkins University Press.

Escobar, A. (2001) Culture sits in places: Reflections on globalism and subaltern strategies of localization. *Political Geography* 20, 139–174.

Feld, S. and Basso, K. (1996) *Senses of Place*. Santa Fe, NM, School of American Research Press.

Fleure, H. (1919 [1996]) Human regions, in *Human Geography: An Essential Anthology*, ed. J. Agnew, D. Livingstone, and A. Rogers. Oxford, Blackwell, pp. 385–387.

Forest, B. (1995) West Hollywood as symbol: The significance of place in the construction of a gay identity. *Environment and Planning D: Society and Space* 13, 133–157.

Glacken, C. J. (1967) *Traces on the Rhodian Shore: Nature and Culture in Western Thought from Ancient Times to the End of the Eighteenth Century.* Berkeley, University of California Press.

Hartshorne, R. (1939) *The Nature of Geography; A Critical Survey of Current Thought in the Light of the Past.* Lancaster, Pa., The Association of American Geographers.

Hartshorne, R. (1959) *Perspective on the Nature of Geography.* Chicago, Rand McNally for the Association of American Geographers.

Harvey, D. (1996) *Justice, Nature and the Geography of Difference.* Cambridge, Mass., Blackwell Publishers.

Heidegger, M. (1962) *Being and Time.* New York, Harper.

Heidegger, M. (1971) Building dwelling thinking, in *Poetry Language Thought.* New York, Harper and Row, pp. 145–161.

Heidegger, M. (1993) *Basic Writings: From Being and Time (1927) to the Task of Thinking (1964).* San Francisco, HarperSanFrancisco.

Herbertson, A. (1905) The major natural regions: An essay in systematic geography. *Geographical Journal* 25, 300–312.

hooks, b. (1990) *Yearning: Race, Gender, and Cultural Politics.* Boston, South End Press.

Jones, M. and MacLeod, G. (2004) Regional spaces, spaces of regionalism: territory, insurgent politics and the English question. *Transactions of the Institute of British Geographers* 29, 433–452.

Kwon, M. (2002) *One Place after Another: Site-Specific Art and Locational Identity.* Cambridge, Mass., MIT Press.

Ley, D. (1977) Social geography and the taken-for-granted world. *Transactions of the Institute of British Geographers* 2, 498–512.

Lösch, A. (1954) *The Economics of Location.* New Haven, Conn., Yale University Press.

Low, S. M. and Lawrence-Zuniga, D. (2002) *The Anthropology of Space and Place: A Reader.* Oxford, Blackwell.

Lukerman, F. (1964) Geography as a formal intellectual discipline and the way in which it contributes to human knowledge. *Canadian Geographer* 8, 167–172.

Malkki, L. (1992) National geographic: The rooting of peoples and the territorialization of national identity among scholars and refugees. *Cultural Anthropology* 7, 24–44.

Malpas, J. E. (n.d.) Thinking topographically: Place, space and geography. Online. Available at http://jeffmalpas.com/wp-content/uploads/2013/02/Thinking-Topographically-Place-Space-and-Geography.pdf (accessed 5 May 2014).

Malpas, J. E. (1999) *Place and Experience: A Philosophical Topography.* Cambridge, Cambridge University Press.

Malpas, J. E. (2006) *Heidegger's Topology: Being, Place, World.* Cambridge, Mass., MIT Press.

Martin, G. J., James, P. E. and James, E. W. (1993) *All Possible Worlds: A History of Geographical Ideas*. New York, Wiley & Sons.

Massey, D. (2005) *For Space*. London, SAGE.

Ogden, L. (2011) *Swamplife: People, Gators, and Mangroves Entangled in the Everglades*. Minneapolis, University of Minnesota Press.

Paasi, A. (2002) Place and region: regional worlds and words. *Progress in Human Geography* 26, 802–811.

Pred, A. R. (1984) Place as historically contingent process: Structuration and the time-geography of becoming places. *Annals of the Association of American Geographers* 74, 279–297.

Price, P. L. (2004) *Dry Place: Landscapes of Belonging and Exclusion*. Minneapolis, University of Minnesota Press.

Prieto, E. (2013) *Literature, Geography, and the Postmodern Poetics of Place*. New York, Palgrave Macmillan.

Relph, E. (1976) *Place and Placelessness*. London, Pion.

Rose, G. (1993) *Feminism and Geography: The Limits of Geographical Knowledge*. Cambridge, Polity.

Sack, R. D. (1992) *Place, Modernity, and the Consumer's World: A Relational Framework For Geographical Analysis*. Baltimore, Johns Hopkins University Press.

Sack, R. D. (1997) *Homo Geographicus* Baltimore, Johns Hopkins University Press.

Sauer, C. O. and Leighly, J. (1963) *Land and Life; A Selection from the Writings of Carl Ortwin Sauer*. Berkeley, University of California Press.

Seamon, D. (1979) *A Geography of the Lifeworld: Movement, Rest, and Encounter*. New York, St. Martin's Press.

Tuan, Y.-F. (1974a) Space and place: Humanistic perspective. *Progress in Human Geography* 6, 211–252.

Tuan, Y.-F. (1974b) *Topophilia: A Study of Environmental Perception, Attitudes, and Values*. Englewood Cliffs, NJ, Prentice-Hall.

Tuan, Y.-F. (1977) *Space and Place: The Perspective of Experience*. Minneapolis, University of Minnesota Press.

Tuan, Y.-F. (1991) A view of geography. *Geographical Review* 81, 99–107.

Vidal de la Blache, P. (1908) *Tableaux de la géographie de la France*. Paris, Librairie Hachette.

Wagner, P. L. and Mikesell, M. W. (1962) *Readings in Cultural Geography*. Chicago, University of Chicago Press.

Williams, R. (1985) *Keywords: A Vocabulary of Culture and Society*. New York, Oxford University Press.

3

Place in a Mobile World

In the previous chapter we traced the development of place as a concept from its origins in Greek philosophy through to the recent development of assemblage theory. A question that arises throughout this history, and one that seems particularly important in today's mobile and globalized world, is how the idea of place (and actual places) is related to the idea of mobility (and actual mobilities). Place appears to involve some notion of stability and permanence while mobility appears to necessitate constant change and process. This chapter considers some of the ways in which place has been conceptualized in relation to mobility, process, and flow. In the first section we will consider how mobilities that are internal to a place help to produce a sense of place. The things we do (practice) create a place that is always being produced and reproduced in a mobile, rather than a static, way. As the chapter progresses we will explore the potential threats to place from mobilities that are beyond it and pass through it, leading some to suggest the end of place as the bedrock of identity and the rise of placelessness, non-place, and the space of flows.

Place, Practice, and Process

Tuan and Relph were not the only geographers who looked to phenomenology in order to develop notions of place. Other "humanistic" geographers, such as David Seamon were keen to arrive, through phenomenological enquiry, at the essence of geographical phenomena. Place was the central

Place: An Introduction, Second Edition. Tim Cresswell.
© 2015 John Wiley & Sons, Ltd. Published 2015 by John Wiley & Sons, Ltd.

concept but, in Seamon's case, bodily mobility, rather than rootedness and authenticity, was the key component to the understanding of place. Following the French philosopher Maurice Merleau-Ponty, Seamon fixed on the "everyday movement in space" – "*any spatial displacement of the body or bodily part initiated by the person himself.* Walking to the mailbox, driving home, going from house to garage, reaching for scissors in a drawer – all these behaviors are examples of movement" (Seamon 1980, 148). As a phenomenological geographer, Seamon was keen to discover the essential experiential character of place through movement. He wanted to transcend specific examples and provide a general account of place as it is embodied.

> Phenomenology…asks if from the variety of ways which men and women behave in and experience their everyday world there are particular patterns which transcend specific empirical contexts and point to the essential human condition – the irreducible crux of people's life-situations which remains when all non-essentials – cultural context, historical era, personal idiosyncracies – are stripped bare through phenomenological procedures. (Seamon 1980, 149)

Seamon believed that most everyday movement takes the form of habit. People drive the same route to work and back every day without thinking about it. People who have moved house find themselves going to their old house and only realize it when they arrive at the door. People reach for scissors in the drawer while engaging in conversation. Such movements appear to be below the level of conscious scrutiny. The body-subject knows what it is doing – there is an

> inherent capacity of the body to direct behaviors of the person intelligently, and thus function as a special kind of subject which expresses itself in a preconscious way usually described by such words as "automatic," "habitual," "involuntary," and "mechanical." (Seamon 1980, 155)

Seamon invokes the metaphor of dance in order to describe the sequence of preconscious actions used to complete a particular task such as washing the dishes. He calls such a sequence a body-ballet. When such movements are sustained though a considerable length of time he calls it a "time–space routine." This describes the habits of a person as they follow a routine path through the day – driving to work, leaving the kids at school, going to lunch, etc. Seamon also looks beyond the individual body movement to group behavior. When many time–space routines are combined within a particular location a "place-ballet" emerges which generates, in Seamon's view, a strong sense of place. The mobilities of bodies combine in space and time to produce an existential insideness – a feeling of belonging within the rhythm of life in place.

A "place-ballet" is an evocative metaphor for our experience of place. It suggests that places are performed on a daily basis through people living their everyday life. Seamon, clearly shares with Relph the notion of being an "insider" or "outsider" in a place but the way someone becomes an insider is more specific. It is through participating in these daily perform-ances that we get to know a place and feel part of it. It also suggests that those who do not know the routine will appear clumsy and "out-of-place" simply through the nonconformity of their bodily practice.

The idea of a sense of place being generated by mobilities which are internal to it is not unique to David Seamon or even to geography. There are a number of instances where writers have evoked a unique sense of place through elaborate descriptions of the ways in which bodies move in and through a particular place. One of the most notable of these is the account of Lower Manhattan's Hudson Street by the urbanist Jane Jacobs in her book *The Death and Life of Great American Cities*. Jacobs was responding to another kind of mobility – the proposed highways that the planner Robert Moses was intending to build through Lower Manhattan. Like Seamon, she uses the metaphor of dance in her account of a "sidewalk ballet" – a spontaneous and complicated choreography that brought its own kind of order to the neighborhood:

> When I get home from work, the ballet is reaching its crescendo. This is the time of roller skates and stilts and tricycles, the games in the lee of the stoop with bottletops and plastic cowboys; this is the time of bundles and packages, zigzagging from the drug store to the fruit stand and back over to the butcher's; this is the time when teen-agers, all dressed up, are pausing to ask if their slips show or their collars look right; this is the time when beautiful girls get out of MG's; this is the time when the fire engines go through; this is the time when anybody you know around Hudson Street will go by. (Jacobs 1961, 52)

The urban theorist Henri Lefebvre was interested in the way rhythm is produced in the modern city. He contrasted the rhythm of the body with the rhythm demanded by an advanced urban capitalist society. He illus-trates this with a description of a square in Paris seen from a high window.

The noise grows, grows in intensity and strength, at its peak becomes unbearable, though quite well borne by the stench of fumes. Then stop. Let's do it again, with more pedestrians. Two minute intervals. Amidst the fury of the cars, the pedestrians cluster together, a clot here, a lump over there; grey dominates, with multicoloured flecks, and these heaps break apart for the race ahead. Sometimes, the old cars stall in the middle of the road and the pedestrians move around them like waves around a rock, though not without condemning the rivers of the badly placed vehicles with withering looks. Hard rhythms; alternations of silence and outburst, time both broken and accentuated, striking he who takes to listening from his window, which astonishes him more than the disparate movements of the crowds. (Lefebvre 2004)

Lefebvre's account of a square in Paris is a little less rosy than Jacobs's of a street in Manhattan, more focused on the hard edge of imposed rhythms. Both accounts, however, reveal the ways in which the mobilities of bodies internal to a place constitute a sense of place. In this sense place and mobility are not antithetical but co-constitutive.

Clearly the things people do in place – the practices that, in turn, produce a lively sense of place – are not always the result of free will. Some actions are freer than others and it is therefore necessary to take into account restraints on action that are the product of social hierarchies and power relations within society. This was part of Lefebvre's point in his account of the production of rhythm in urban space. A given social order, he argues, imposes its rhythms on to the bodies of people. The fine balancing of constraint and freedom also became the subject of geographers influenced by structuration theory – particularly the work of Anthony Giddens and Pierre Bourdieu. In his paper "Place as historically contingent process" (Pred 1984) Allan Pred announces his dissatisfaction with the prevailing notions of place at the time. He argues that place is too often thought of (by some) in terms of fixed visible and measurable attributes (this many houses, that population, these amenities). As such they become "little more than frozen scenes for human activity" (Pred 1984, 279). Humanistic geographers do not escape his critical comments as they too "conceive of place as an inert, experienced scene" (Pred 1984, 279). Pred argues instead for a notion of place that emphasizes change and process. Places are never "finished" but always "becoming." Place is "what takes place ceaselessly, what contributes to history in a specific context through the creation and utilization of a physical setting" (Pred 1984, 279). This approach is informed by structuration theory – a set of ideas primarily associated with the British sociologist Anthony Giddens.

Structuration theory attempts to describe and understand the relations between the overarching structures that influence our lives (ranging from big structures such as capitalism and patriarchy to smaller-scale structures such as national and local institutions) and our own ability to exercise agency in our everyday lives. Structurationists say that our actions are neither determined by structures above and beyond us, nor completely the product of free will. Structures depend on our actions to exist and our actions are given meaning by the structures that lie beyond them. Think of language for example. A language such as English clearly provides a structure of vocabulary and grammar. Stray too far from these rules and we cease to make sense. Having said that, no use of language is entirely the product of rules. People use language in different ways. Sometimes this usage does not comply with rules. If this happens often enough the structure of language itself begins to change. Without the structure, the individual use of language would have no meaning – in this sense structure enables. Without people practicing the language, the structure would be no structure at all – it would be a dead language.

Now think of this in terms of place. We clearly inhabit material landscapes that, excepting rare instances, we had little say in constructing. These landscapes have walls, doors, windows, spaces of flow (roads, paths, bridges, etc.) that we have to negotiate in order to live. We cannot walk through walls and we are unlikely to wander down the middle of the road without endangering our lives. Places also have less concrete structures. Laws and rules pervade place. We cannot park on a double yellow line (in the UK) or by a fire hydrant (in the US) without risking a fine. We cannot enter private property at will. We are supposed to be at work by nine o'clock. And there are also sets of cultural and social expectations that pervade places. We should not talk loudly to ourselves in public. Women are discouraged from walking alone down dark alleys at night. Young men are not supposed to gather at street corners. All of these structures very from place to place and when we travel we are expected to familiarize ourselves with them.

At a given moment in time, place provides a geographically specific set of structures. But even with layer upon layer of structuring conditions no one can safely predict what you or I are going to do. We might skip work (or a lecture) and call in sick. The places we have to negotiate are the result of the practices of those who were here before us, but this place in the future will be different. It is not a once and for all achieved state. Think of a new green rectangle of lawn in a town or city somewhere. Trees are planted in the middle and two footpaths meet in the exact center to divide the lawn

ticed can help us think of place in radically open and non-essentialized ways, where place is constantly struggled over and reimagined in practical ways. Place is the raw material for the creative production of identity rather than an a priori label of identity. Place provides the conditions of possibility for creative social practice.

Place, Openness, and Change

The kind of place at the center of much of humanistic geography is very much a place of rootedness and authenticity. In David Harvey's discussion of place this meaning is retained but becomes a symbol of reactionary exclusivity. As long as place signifies a tight and relatively immobile connection between a group of people and a site then it will be constantly implicated in the construction of "us" (people who belong in a place) and "them" (people who do not). In this way outsiders are constructed. In Harvey's work this produces a fairly damning critique of place as it is normally understood (see Chapter 4 for more on this).

But place need not be thought of in such introverted and exclusionary terms. We saw, in Chapter 2, how places gather or assemble elements from a world that lies beyond it. In this sense, place is both unique and relational. Doreen Massey rejects this notion of an introverted place in her development of the idea of a "progressive" or "global" sense of place. She has encouraged us to think of place in a way that combines bodies, objects, and flows in new ways. As Arturo Escobar has argued "places gather things, thoughts, and memories in particular configurations" (Escobar 2001, 143). Place in this sense becomes an event rather than a secure ontological thing rooted in notions of the authentic. Place as an event is marked by openness and change rather than boundedness and permanence. This significantly alters the value put on place as it is constructed from the outside rather from the inside. We will consider Massey's important definition of a "global (or progressive) sense of place" in the next chapter in more depth. But she is not the only one considering how places are constructed by objects and processes from outside.

The artist and commentator Lucy Lippard has made similar observations in her book *The Lure of the Local*.

> Inherent in the local is the concept of place – a portion of land/town/cityscape seen from the inside, the resonance of a specific location that is known

and familiar…Place is latitudinal and longitudinal within the map of a person's life. It is temporal and spatial, personal and political. A layered location replete with human histories and memories, place has width as well as depth. It is about connections, what surrounds it, what formed it, what happened there, what will happen there. (Lippard 1997, 7)

Here Lippard agrees with Massey's contention that places are "about connections" but makes more of the layering of histories which sediment in place and become the bedrock for future action.

Environmental historians have also developed ways of thinking about place that mesh well with Massey's progressive sense of place. William Cronon's book *Nature's Metropolis*, for instance, reveals how Chicago was constructed through its relationship with a rural hinterland (Cronon 1991). Cronon traces the voyages of corn, timber, meat, and other products from the countryside into the metropolis and shows how the movements in and out of place produce new material landscapes, new sets of social relations, and new relations between people and "nature." He performs a similar analysis of a small ghost town in Alaska in a wonderful essay called "Kennecott journey: The paths out of town."

In his essay Cronon visits Kennecott, a long deserted town north of Valdez in South Central Alaska. He describes the ruins of place in great detail – particularly its huge, spectacularly rambling crushing mill that provided so much employment for its earlier residents.

It is a ghost factory in a ghost town, yet its haunting could almost have begun yesterday. In the bunkhouse where the millmen slept and ate, linen is still on the beds, and plates are still on the cafeteria tables. Open account books lie scattered around the store-rooms and offices, protected from decay only by the coldness of the northern climate. Even the machinery is remarkably well preserved: Lift the gears of the sifting mechanisms, and beautifully clear oil still bathes the gears with lubricant. (Cronon 1992, 30)

Cronon's essay explores what made this place a booming and vibrant town for a little more than thirty years and what subsequently led to its downfall. In order to do this he traces the links between Kennecott and other places. Between 1911 and 1938 Kennecott thrived because of the copper that had been discovered there – the richest vein the world had ever seen. The 1930s saw the bottom fall out of the copper market and the rich vein of copper was, anyway, beginning to yield less material. In 1938 the Kennecott Copper

Company closed all its Alaskan mines and moved operations to other sites in North and South America.

"What" Cronon asks "is one to make of this place and of the memories that lie so visibly on the landscape?" (Cronon 1992, 32). His answer is to trace the connections between Kennecott and the rest of the world. These connections include

> the ecology of people as organisms sharing the universe with many other organisms, the political economy of people as social beings reshaping nature and one another to produce their collective life, and the cultural values of people as storytelling creatures struggling to find meaning of their place in the world…
>
> As we seek to understand Kennecott, the questions we ask must show us the paths out of town – the connections between this lonely place and the rest of the world – for only by walking those paths can we reconnect his ghost community to the circumstances that created it. (Cronon 1992, 32, 33)

There are many "paths out of town." One is that produced by the need to eat food in a place that does not provide much sustenance. As soon as there were significant numbers of non-native people in Kennecott then food had to be imported.

> When people exchange things in their immediate vicinity for things that can only be obtained elsewhere, they impose a new set of meanings on the local landscape and connect it to the wider world. These increase the chance that the local environment will begin to change in response to outside forces, so that trade becomes a powerful new source of ecological change. (Cronon 1992, 37)

Kennecott soon became part of ever-wider networks of exchange. Russian traders started to operate along the coast of Alaska and thus integrated even interior Alaska into a large Eurasian market for furs.

> Trade linked the resources of one ecosystem with the human demands of another. Alaskan villages that had no sugar, alcohol, or tobacco obtained such things by trading with communities that had no furs. The net result was to redefine the resources of the Alaskan landscape, pushing them beyond the needs of the local subsistence into the realm of the market, where any good could be transformed into any other. At the same time the act of economic consumption came to be increasingly separated from the place of ecological production, distancing people from the consequences of their own acts and desires. (Cronon 1992, 38–39)

Cronon traces the development of trade between the native population and the arriving military expeditions. The key resource, of course, was copper. While the native population of Kennecott saw copper as interesting for its color and the fact that they could make it into weapons, tools, and jewelry they were not aware of its ability to conduct electricity and had little idea of its value to American industry. The huge mines of Kennecott and the town that surrounded it were focused on this resource. Along with the new population came new foods and plant species such as turnips and cabbages. Local game was soon hunted to exhaustion. Food was a problem. In order to supply the growing population with nutrition a railroad was built. In order for the new population to mine the copper they had to import new definitions of property – thus a legal landscape was imported along with the turnips. The native population had no concept of static property or place. They were nomadic and would move according to the availability of resources. This lifestyle, Cronon writes, "left them little concerned with drawing sharp property boundaries upon the landscape"; the newcomers "had in mind a completely different way of owning and occupying the terrain. And therein lay the origin of the community called Kennecott" (Cronon 1992, 42). So the irony of Kennecott – a place produced by its connections – was that a new idea of place itself was imported from outside. Place based on property and boundaries.

To understand the place called Kennecott, and by extension any place, Cronon argues, we must pay attention to its connections. Kennecott became possible at the moment it appeared because connections made it possible. Everything the residents consumed depended upon a prior history in other places from the development of salmon canneries on the Alaskan shoreline to the coffee and sugar trade with the tropics.

> At no prior moment in the history of the West would it have been possible for capitalists in New York to hire engineers and workers in Alaska to construct a railroad, mine, and crushing mill deep in the interior of that remote territory so that the nation's cities could purchase a metal they hardly knew they needed just a half century before. (Cronon 1992, 49)

Similarly the demise of Kennecott owes everything to the emergence of cheaper copper industries in South America and the dictates and foibles of a truly global economy.

Cronon's work is not written as theory. Like many environmental historians he uses narrative to make us think about the issues at hand. But what his journey to Kennecott tells us is that places need to be understood as sites that are connected to others around the world in constantly evolving networks which are social, cultural, and natural/environmental. Places need to be understood through the paths that lead in and out. Similar stories could be written about many, if not all, places around the world and geographers have begun to think in very similar terms. Matthew Gandy has explored how New York City has been constructed through its relationship to nature (Gandy 2002) and Daniel Clayton has explored the construction of British Columbia through the passages of a whole array of imperial and local travelers to and through the place (Clayton 2000).

The End of Place?

The very processes Cronon writes about – the way in which places are tied into global flows of people, meanings and things – have led some to perceive an accelerating erosion of place. A combination of mass communication, increased mobility, and a consumer society has been blamed for a rapidly accelerating homogenization of the world. More and more of our lives, it has been argued, take place in spaces that could be anywhere – that look, feel, sound, and smell the same wherever in the globe we may be. Fast food outlets, shopping malls, airports, high street shops, and hotels are all arguably more or less the same wherever we go. These are spaces that seem detached from the local environment and tell us nothing about the particular locality in which they are located. The meaning that provides the sense of attachment to place has been radically thinned out.

This issue of the erosion of place was a central theme of humanistic geographer Edward Relph's book *Place and Placelessness* (Relph 1976). Relph, you will recall, was one of the geographers who brought the issue of place to the attention of geographers in a sustained way. Bear in mind that he was writing long before the level of geographical homogenization we (in the West) now experience was quite so ubiquitous. Relph was concerned that it was becoming increasingly difficult for people to feel connected to the world through place. Relph makes the distinction between the experience of insideness and outsideness in the human experience of place. "To be inside a place is to belong to it and identify with it, and the more profoundly inside you are the stronger is the identity with the place" (Relph 1976, 49). At the opposite extreme, existential outsideness involves the alienation from place which is the antithesis of an unreflective sense of belonging that comes from being an existential insider.

A key term for Relph (developing Heidegger's notion of "dwelling") is "authenticity." Authenticity means a genuine and sincere attitude; "As a form of existence authenticity consists of a complete awareness and acceptance of responsibility for your own existence" (Relph 1976, 78). An existential insider has an authentic attitude to a place which is likely to be authentic. An inauthentic attitude to place, on the other hand,

> is essentially no sense of place, for it involves no awareness of the deep and symbolic significances of places and no appreciation of their identities. It is merely an attitude which is socially convenient and acceptable – an uncritically accepted stereotype, an intellectual or aesthetic fashion that can be adopted without real involvement. (Relph 1976, 82)

In the modern world, Relph argues, we are surrounded by a general condition of creeping placelessness, marked by an inability to have authentic relationships to place because the new placelessness does not allow people to become existential insiders.

> An inauthentic attitude towards places is transmitted through a number of processes, or perhaps more accurately "media," which directly or indirectly encourage "placelessness," that is, a weakening of the identity of places to the point where they not only look alike but feel alike and offer the same bland possibilities for experience. (Relph 1976, 90)

The processes that lead to this are various and include the ubiquity of mass communication and culture as well as big business and central authority. Tourism, Relph writes, is particularly to blame as it encourages the Disney-fication, museumization, and futurization of places.

One of the main culprits here is mobility. Relph makes a direct connection between inauthentic placelessness and mobility by claiming that the mobility of American homeowners (changing home every three years) reduces the significance of home and thus plays a major role in the growing problem of placelessness in the (American) modern world. Another factor in the creation of placelessness is, in Relph's view, modern travel/tourism which encourages a fascination with the "machinery and paraphernalia of travel...itself. In short, where someone goes is less important than the act and style of going" (Relph 1976, 87). A place like Disneyland represents the

Figure 3.2 Cinderella's Castle at Walt Disney World, Orlando, Florida. Authors have argued that tourist places such as Disney World are not real places but "place-less" places or "pseudo-places" with no real history and no sense of belonging. Source: photo by SteamFan (own work (Nikon D80)) [GFDL (http://www.gnu.org/copyleft/fdl.html), CC-BY-SA-3.0 (http://creativecommons.org/licenses/by-sa/3.0/) or CC-BY-2.5 (http://creativecommons.org/licenses/by/2.5)], via Wikimedia Commons.

epitome of placelessness constructed, as it is, purely for outsiders and now reproduced across the globe in France, China, and Japan.

Superhighways also play their part in the destruction of place as they do not connect places and are separated from the surrounding landscape – they "start everywhere and lead nowhere" (Relph 1976, 90). Before the highways the railways were the culprits destroying authentic senses of place:

> Roads, railways, airports, cutting across or imposed on the landscape rather than developing with it, are not only features of placelessness in their own

right, but, by making possible the mass movement of people with all their fashions and habits, have encouraged the spread of placelessness well beyond their immediate impacts. (Relph 1976, 90)

Relph connects various forms of increased mobility to what he calls "mass culture" and mass values which again dilute authentic relations to place. Places become "other directed" and more alike across a globe of transient connections. Mobility and mass culture lead to irrational and shallow landscapes.

In a similar way the anthropologist Marc Augé has argued that the facts of postmodernity (he refers to supermodernity) point to a need for a radical rethinking of the notion of place (Augé 1995). Place, he argues, has traditionally been thought of as a fantasy of a "society anchored since time immemorial in the permanence of an intact soil." Augé's argument is that such places are receding in importance and being replaced by "non-places."

The multiplication of what we may call empirical non-places is characteristic of the contemporary world. Spaces of circulation (freeways, airways), consumption (department stores, supermarkets), and communication (telephones, faxes, television, cable networks) are taking up more room all over the earth today. They are spaces where people coexist or cohabit without living together. (Augé 1995, 110).

Non-places are sites marked by their transience – the preponderance of mobility. Augé's use of the term "non-place" does not have the same negative moral connotations as Relph's "placelessness." By non-place Augé is referring to sites marked by the "fleeting, the temporary and ephemeral." Non-places include freeways, airports, supermarkets – sites where particular histories and traditions are not (allegedly) relevant, unrooted places marked by mobility and travel. Non-place is essentially the space of travelers. Augé's arguments force theorists of culture to reconsider the theory and method of their disciplines. While conventionally figured places demand thoughts which reflect assumed boundaries and traditions, non-places demand new mobile ways of thinking.

Tuan, too, reflects on the effects of a mobile world on the experience of place in modernity. He picks out the figure of the businessman as a symbol of this new world:

He moves around so much that places for him tend to lose their special character. What are his significant places? The home is in the suburb. He

Figure 3.3 Widecombe-in-the-Moor, a village on Dartmoor, England. When people think and write about place they often fix on old small places that seem "authentic" such as this village on Dartmoor. Think, for instance, of the way Heidegger wrote about a cabin in the Black Forest to make his argument about "being-in-the-world." Source: photo by Manfred Heyde (Own work) [GFDL (http://www.gnu.org/copyleft/fdl.html) or CC-BY-SA-3.0-2.5-2.0-1.0 (http://creativeco mmons.org/licenses/by-sa/3.0)], via Wikimedia Commons.

lives there, but home is not wholly divorced from work. It is occasionally a showplace for the lavish entertainment of colleagues and business associates...The executive takes periodic trips abroad, combining business with pleasure. He stays at the same hotel, or with the same friends, in Milan, and again in Barbados. The circuits of movement are complex. (Tuan 1977, 183)

This kind of life, Tuan goes on, leads inevitably to a superficial sense of place:

Abstract knowledge *about* a place can be acquired in short order if one is diligent. The visual quality of an environment is quickly tallied if one has the artist's eye. But the "feel" of a place takes longer to acquire. It is made up of experiences, mostly fleeting and undramatic, repeated day after day and over the span of years. (Tuan 1977, 183)

Figure 3.4   Chhatrapari Shivaji Airport, Mumbai. Airports, by contrast, are frequently described as non-places or placeless. They do not appear to have histories
and are marked by transience and mobility. Source: photo by Alex Graves from
Lugano, Switzerland (Mumbai Airport) [CC-BY-SA-2.0 (http://creativecommons.
org/licenses/by-sa/2.0)], via Wikimedia Commons.

Nigel Thrift describes mobility as a structure of feeling that emerged with
modernity and attained new characteristics as we approached the twenty-
first century. The focus of his argument is on developing technologies and
"machine complexes" starting with the stagecoach and ending (provision-
ally) with the Internet. By 1994, when he wrote the essay, developments in
speed, light, and power had reached such a point that they had combined
and fused with people and changed everything. Towards the end of his
essay he lays out some of the consequences of this structure of feeling for
human geography. One of these concerns place.

> What is place in this "in-between" world? The short answer is – compro-
> mised: permanently in a state of enunciation, between addresses, always
> deferred. Place are "stages of intensity." Traces of movement, speed and cir-

culation. One might read this depiction of "almost places"…in Baudrillard-ean terms as a world of third-order simulacra, where encroaching pseudo-places have finally advanced to eliminate places altogether. Or one might record places…as strategic installations, fixed addresses that capture traffic. Or, finally, one might read them…as frames for varying practices of space, time and speed. (Thrift 1994, 212–213)

Gone are the implicit moral judgments of inauthenticity and lack of commitment. At worst this reading of mobility and place is neutral and at best it is a positive celebration of mobile worlds. Thrift sees mobility as a mark of all of life in an increasingly speeded-up world. The study of the modern world is a study of velocities and vectors. Rather than comparing mobility to place, mobilities are placed in relation to each other. Place in this world seems increasingly redundant.

Place, Identity, and Mobility

A similar set of arguments has arisen in work on the relation between cultural identity and place. Augé's thesis of non-place as a new kind of spatial arena, distinct from the deep map of anthropological place, is mirrored in the work of anthropologists and others who locate the production of identities in cosmopolitan forms of mobility rather than in stable and bounded places. Terms such as the "transnational," the "diasporic," the "hybrid," and the "cosmopolitan" all imply a critique of views which suggest that identities are formed in specific places (Malkki 1992, Hannerz 1990, Gupta and Ferguson 1992, Jackson *et al.* 2004). To take just "cosmopolitanism" as an example, it is consistently argued that this is a form of identity that is characteristic of increasing numbers of people in the twenty-first century and that it is based on mobility, communication, and a diverse set of allegiances to more than one place. Consider the following assertion that appears in a paper about Indian call-centers and a number of short films that portray the call-center workers as stationary but cosmopolitan people.

Discourses of cosmopolitanism evoke ways of being and acting beyond the local, of having affective attachments in multiple spaces beyond the boundaries of the resident nation-state. Indeed the call center-agents and actors who portray them inhabit multiple places simultaneously, and have imaginary investments in places that transcend and transgress their immediate environs. (Menon 2013, 162)

Cosmopolitanism often appears as something worthy of celebration – an escape from the narrow parochialism of place and the local. Cosmopolitans belong to a world culture and are keen to engage with the "other." Often, as in Ulf Hannerz's work, the "cosmopolitan" is contrasted with the "local." An equation that is repeated again and again links cosmopolitanism to a new global elite while the poor remain local. "The rich have mobility and the poor have locality…the rich are global and the poor are local" writes Terry Eagleton (Eagleton 2003, 22) echoing Manuel Castells three years earlier who wrote "elites are cosmopolitan, people are local" (Castells 2000, 446). These two (remarkably similar) quotes make some sense when you first encounter them. Castells is arguing that some people are able to travel more or less at will (along with capital and information) and that the poor resist this world of flows through embedding themselves in place. That place is all they have. The poor can practice what David Harvey calls *militant particularism* (Harvey 1996).

But on another level this insistence is strange. I presume Eagleton and Castells are well traveled. Even if they only travel as much as I do they are well traveled. They inhabit the skin of the cosmopolitan elite in some sense. I do this too. When I travel I encounter (for instance) taxi drivers from Ethiopia and Somalia. When I am in my hotel I cannot help but notice that the people cleaning the room for me are almost always Eastern European or from Southeast Asia. They appear to speak multiple languages and have relatives in London. The poor seem to be pretty mobile and far more cosmopolitan than us, the kinetic elite. The English-speaking academics and business people who flit around the world rarely speak the number of languages spoken by their supposedly immobile and non-cosmopolitan underlings who drive them places and clean their rooms. They may cover more miles but in many ways they travel less. It is the different ways in which they move that need to be attended to.

The concept of cosmopolitanism is one of many that mobilizes identity. It suggests the decreasing relevance of place in a modern world marked by mobility and flow. To Augé this is expressed through the spread of non-place. For Castells it is the rise of a "space of flows" and the erosion of a "space of places." A more sophisticated reading, however, leaves room for the continuing salience of place, even in a mobile world. For one thing, the cosmopolitans need the locals to exist in order to be able to enjoy their encounters with difference. In a more nuanced version of the "elites are cosmopolitan, the poor are local" argument, Hannerz makes the following point.

Here, however, today's cosmopolitans and locals have common interests in the survival of cultural diversity. For the latter, diversity itself, as a matter of personal access to varied cultures, may be of little intrinsic interest. It just so happens that this is the principle which allows all locals to stick to their respective cultures. For the cosmopolitans, in contrast, there is value in diversity as such, but they are not likely to get it, in anything like the present form, unless other people are allowed to carve out special niches for their cultures, and keep them. Which is to say that there can be no cosmopolitans without locals. (Hannerz 1990)

In other words, the cosmopolitan identity may be formed through mobility and a decrease in the importance of one's own place, but it simultaneously depends on continued variation in the world – the existence of recognizably different places inhabited by "locals." At the same time it has become possible to be cosmopolitan without moving at all as so much "difference" can be experienced through the world coming *to* the inhabitants of a major city. The workers in Indian call-centers, for instance, are remarkably cosmopolitan in a way that is quite different from the global mobile elite (Menon 2013). Such people mark a disconnection between the idea of cosmopolitanism and the global elite. They mark the possibility of a "cosmopolitanism from below" formed both in particular places and through the travels of a global underclass – the vagabonds who serve the tourists in the terms of the sociologist Zygmunt Bauman (Kurasawa 2004, Bauman 1998).

Place is also shown to have continuing salience in a mobile world in the work of the anthropologist Anna Tsing. In her book *Friction: An Ethnography of Global Connection*, Tsing considers the global spread of ideas and things considered to be *universal*. Globalization relies on the global spread of science, capital, and political ideologies such as liberal democracy. These are supposed to flow freely over the surface of the Earth, binding wherever they touch to a globally uniform system. Through an ethnography of the logging industry in the Indonesian rainforest, Tsing shows how these mobile universals are transformed as they engage with the particularities of place – what she calls the "sticky materiality of practical encounters" (Tsing 2005, 1). Things such as science, capital, and liberal democracy are supposed to be marked by their objective status – linked to nowhere in particular. It is particularity that they are supposed to be opposed to. And yet, Tsing suggests, they have to engage with the particularity of place in order to get purchase on the world. To be universal, capital (for instance) has to be everywhere. But to be everywhere it has to spread and become material. To do this it has to emerge in the particular – in place. Tsing refers to this as friction – the moment when a *universal* encounters the particularity of place and has to transform itself in order to take form in the world. Universals such as science and capital are, by necessity, mobile and global – they are key elements in the process of globalization from above. But to become global they have to touch down and make contact with actually existing places. Mobile universals encounter the friction of place, giving the universals shape and efficacy. "Engaged universals must convince us to pay attention to them," Tsing writes. "*All* universals are engaged when considered as practical projects accomplished in an heterogeneous world" (Tsing 2005, 8). Place provides friction. The idea of friction forces us to pay attention to the forces we need to move. While mobility (particularly global mobility) is often considered to be frictionless – and antithetical to place – it is actually friction (and thus place) that makes mobility possible. Try walking on a frictionless surface – it cannot happen. Universals such as capital and science, Tsing shows us, can only experience becoming through the way in which they are made particular through friction and in place.

Conclusion

This chapter has considered the role of place in a mobile world. We live in a world in which the "end of geography" has frequently been heralded. Leaving aside the fact that mobility is every bit as geographical as place, this seems to suggest that place (as well as things such as nation-states and borders) has become less important as the world has become more connected and more mobile. This is not the case. Mobility has always been part of place. At a micro-scale, as we saw at the beginning of the chapter, bodily mobilities are a key constituent in the production of senses of place. But even at a larger scale mobilities always have to exist in relation to places. Similarly, places are produced, through mobilities, by their connections to a world beyond.

In addition to these largely theory-driven observations, it is possible to see the continued salience of place all around us. Just when place (at least in the form of relatively stable wholes firmly rooted in the past) appears to be more or less irrelevant, it seems to be the word on many people's lips. Advertisers sell us places or ways to make places. Travel brochures encourage us to get to know places. Politicians and artists lament the loss of place and strive to produce new ones. Writers of creative non-fiction have been at the center of a cottage industry of writing on place. Urban dwellers leave the city to look for a place in the country where life will slow down and they can raise some chickens.

Clearly if place is the very bedrock of our humanity, as some have claimed, then it cannot have vanished because it is a necessary part of the human condition. Places have certainly changed though and this has produced anxiety. Lucy Lippard, a thoughtful writer on place, has reflected on what place might mean in the speeded-up world we inhabit. Here the effect of mobility on place is less extreme than the likes of Relph, Augé, and Thrift, from their varying perspectives, would have us believe.

> Most of us move around a lot, but when we move we often come into contact with those who haven't moved around, or have come from different places. This should give us a better understanding of difference (though it will always be impossible to understand everything about difference). Each time we enter a new place, we become one of the ingredients of an existing hybridity, which is really what all "local places" consist of. (Lippard 1997, 5–6)

Here Lippard suggests that mobility and place go hand in hand as places are always already hybrid anyway. By moving through, between, and around them we are simply adding to the mix. She suggests that the "pull of place" continues to operate in all of us as the "geographical component of the psychological need to belong somewhere, one antidote to a prevailing alienation" (Lippard 1997, 7). Even in the age of a "restless, multitraditional people," she argues, and "even as the power of place is diminished and often lost, it continues – as an absence – to define culture and identity. It also continues – as a presence – to change the way we live" (Lippard 1997, 20).

References

Anderson, B. and Harrison, P. (2010) *Taking-Place: Non-Representational Theories and Geography.* Farnham, Ashgate.

Augé, M. (1995) *Non-Places: Introduction to an Anthropology of Supermodernity.* London and New York, Verso.

Bauman, Z. (1998) *Globalization: The Human Consequences.* New York, Columbia University Press.

Castells, M. (2000) *The Rise of the Network Society.* Oxford, Blackwell.

Certeau, M. de (1984) *The Practice of Everyday Life.* Berkeley, University of California Press.

Clayton, D. W. (2000) *Islands of Truth: The Imperial Fashioning of Vancouver Island.* Vancouver, UBC Press.

Cronon, W. (1991) *Nature's Metropolis: Chicago and the Great West.* New York, Norton.

Cronon, W. (1992) Kennecott journey: The paths out of town, in *Under an Open Sky*, ed. W. Cronon, G. Miles, and J. Gitlin. New York, Norton, pp. 28–51.

Eagleton, T. (2003) *After Theory.* New York, Basic Books.

Escobar, A. (2001) Culture sits in places: Reflections on globalism and subaltern strategies of localization. *Political Geography* 20, 139–174.

Gandy, M. (2002) *Concrete and Clay: Reworking Nature in New York City.* Cambridge, Mass., MIT Press.

Gregory, D. (1998) *Explorations in Critical Human Geography: Hettner Lecture 1997.* Heidelberg, Department of Geography, University of Heidelberg.

Gupta, A. and Ferguson, J. (1992) Beyond culture: Space, identity and the politics of difference. *Cultural Antropology* 7, 6–22.

Hannerz, U. (1990) Cosmopolitans and locals in world culture. *Theory, Culture and Society* 7, 237–251.

Harvey, D. (1996) *Justice, Nature and the Geography of Difference.* Cambridge, Mass., Blackwell Publishers.

Hebdige, D. (1988) *Subculture: The Meaning of Style.* London, Routledge.

Jackson, P., Crang, P., and Dwyer, C. (2004) *Transnational Spaces.* London, Routledge.

Jacobs, J. (1961) *The Death and Life of Great American Cities.* New York, Vintage.

Kurasawa, F. (2004) A cosmopolitanism from below: Alternative globalization and the creation of a solidarity without bounds. *Archives Européennes de Sociologie* 45, 233-+.

Lefebvre, H. (1991) *The Production of Space.* Oxford, Blackwell.

Lefebvre, H. (2004) *Rhythmanalysis: Space, Time, and Everyday Life.* London and New York, Continuum.

Lippard, L. (1997) *The Lure of the Local: Senses of Place in a Multicultural Society.* New York, The New Press.

Malkki, L. (1992) National geographic: The rooting of peoples and the territorialization of national identity among scholars and refugees. *Cultural Anthropology* 7, 24–44.

Menon, J. (2013) Calling local/talking global: The cosmo-politics of the call-center industry. *Women and Performance: A Journal of Feminist Theory* 23, 162–177.

Pred, A. R. (1984) Place as historically contingent process: Structuration and the time-geography of becoming places. *Annals of the Association of American Geographers* 74, 279–297.

Relph, E. (1976) *Place and Placelessness.* London, Pion.

Seamon, D. (1980) Body–subject, time–space routines, and place-ballets, in *The Human Experience of Space and Place*, ed A. Buttimer and D. Seamon. London, Croom Helm, pp. 148–165.

Soja, E. W. (1999) Thirdspace: Expanding the scope of the geographical imagination, in *Human Geography Today*, ed. D. Massey, J. Allen, and P. Sarre. Cambridge, Polity, pp. 260–278.

Thrift, N. (1983) On the determination of social action in time and space. *Environment and Planning D: Society and Space* 1, 23–57.

Thrift, N. (1994) Inhuman geographies: Landscapes of speed, light and power, in *Writing the Rural: Five Cultural Geographies*, ed. P. Cloke. London, Paul Chapman, pp. 191–250.

Thrift, N. (2007) *Non-Representational Theory: Space, Politics, Affect*. London and New York, Routledge.

Tsing, A. L. (2005) *Friction: An Ethnography of Global Connection*. Princeton, NJ, Princeton University Press.

Tuan, Y.-F. (1977) *Space and Place: The Perspective of Experience*. Minneapolis, University of Minnesota Press.

Reading "A Global Sense of Place"

The purpose of this chapter is to consider, in some depth, how place has been thought through in one, particularly influential, reading. Of course there are many possible readings, and many of them have been mentioned in previous chapters. Doreen Massey's paper "A global sense of place" has been widely cited as a plea for a new conceptualization of place as open and hybrid – a product of interconnecting flows – of routes rather than roots. This extroverted notion of place calls into question the whole history of place as a center of meaning connected to a rooted and "authentic" sense of identity forever challenged by mobility. It also makes a critical intervention into widely held notions of the erosion of place through mobility, globalization, and time–space compression (the theme of Chapter 3). I have chosen this paper, then, because it allows for reflection on all of the central themes surrounding the notion of place, and points towards a new way of thinking. Looking at this paper alone, however, would not do justice to the complexity and political urgency of the debates around place. It needs to be understood in its intellectual and historical context. For this reason, this chapter also includes excerpts from David Harvey's chapter "From space to place and back again" in his book *Justice, Nature and the Geography of Difference* (Harvey 1996). Finally a nuanced response to both of these papers is given by Jon May in his paper "Globalization and the politics of place" (May 1996).

Historical Context

"A global sense of place" was published in 1991, in *Marxism Today*, and republished in 1994 in Massey's book *Space, Place, and Gender*. It has also been anthologized in the collection *Reading Human Geography* (Barnes and Gregory 1997) and, in a slightly different form, in the collection *Mapping the Futures* (Bird 1993). This was a time, as Massey writes herself, when the world was experiencing rapid "globalization." Transport, communications, and institutional support for global capital (the World Bank, the International Monetary Fund, etc.) had conspired to seemingly make places less important – less unique. Anti-globalization protests were small and unreported until the latter part of the 1990s. In the UK, more and more people flew abroad for holidays while the high street at home seemed increasingly homogenous as global chains such as McDonald's appeared. Alongside this apparent homogenization, a new kind of diversity was formed in the Western world. Clothes came from around the world (labels read "product of more than one country"), "ethnic" restaurants expanded from the expected Chinese and Indian (in the UK) offerings to include Mexican, Vietnamese, and Mongolian (for instance). Supermarkets displayed a bewildering array of foodstuffs that often needed elaborate explanations on a nearby sign ("how to use a star fruit"). It suddenly became possible to buy 15 varieties of rice from around the world. It seemed that two complementary changes were occurring at a global scale – the repetition of outlets owned by multinational corporations everywhere across the globe (homogenization) and the flowering of a diverse array of international cultural products in urban areas everywhere. Both of these appeared to threaten the notion of unique places.

The early 1990s also witnessed a number of violent place-based uprisings usually fired by the desires of oppressed minorities for nationhood or some other form of regional autonomy. The one most often portrayed in the Western media was the break-up of Yugoslavia and the horrors of ethnic cleansing that accompanied it. This period also saw the rise of Islamic fundamentalism – such as the success of the Taliban in Afghanistan – which was, in part, a reaction to globalization and the perceived cultural imperialism of the United States and Europe. On a smaller scale, the United States, in particular, was witnessing a rapid proliferation of "gated communities" – specially managed places to live with extremely tight security, designed to protect against the imagined horrors of city life (Till 1993). The heritage industry was also active, attempting to package places and their histories in a sanitized way in order to attract tourists and their money. So at many scales, place was very much on the agenda either through its apparent homogenization or through various attempts to create places from the nation to the heritage park.

It was in this context that Doreen Massey and David Harvey engaged in quite different analyses of the idea of place in the contemporary world and what it might mean. As we will see, Harvey, whose paper "From space to place and back again" was first given at a conference at the Tate Gallery, London, in 1990, was quite disturbed by the emergence of a politics of place that could often be quite reactionary and exclusionary – using place to define one group of people over and against others. Massey, on the other hand, sought to redefine place as a much more open and progressive force in the world. We will start with Harvey.

Harvey on Place

David Harvey, in his paper "From space to place and back again," begins with an example from his then home town of Baltimore to make his more abstract arguments about place.

> On Sunday August 14, 1994 a brutal double murder occurred in Guilford. An elderly white couple, both distinguished physicians but now retired in their 80s, were found in their bed bludgeoned to death with a baseball bat. Murder is no stranger to Baltimore (the rate for the city is one a day). But in the eyes of the media the Guilford killings were special. The main local newspaper – the *Baltimore Sun* – devoted full-page coverage to them when most other murders received nominal attention. The media dwelt at length on how this was the third such incident in Guilford in recent months and that something plainly had to be done to protect the community if it was to survive. The solution that had long been pressed by the Guilford Community Association was to turn Guilford into a gated community with restricted access. (Harvey 1996, 292)

Harvey reports how the media turned to the views of Oscar Newman, the author of *Defensible Space* (1972), who suggested that the production of gated communities was one way to secure neighborhoods against crimes such as prostitution, drug dealing, and mugging. Gated communities are essentially collections of houses (and sometimes shops and leisure services) with a wall around them and one or two ways in and out. These entrances/exits can then be policed by private security forces, closed-circuit TV and other forms of surveillance. Residents have passes to allow them in and out and guests are recorded. In the case of Guilford, the production of the gated community would effectively separate a white community (in Guilford) from a black community (beyond).

> The whole tenor of the *Sun's* report implied…that crime was an African-American and "underclass" habit and that therefore the construction of barriers against people of color and of low income, however regrettable, might be justifiable as a means to secure a defensible space of "community" for an affluent white middle-class population that might otherwise flee the city. Place had to be secured against the uncontrolled vectors of spatiality. (Harvey 1996, 292)

As it turned out, the murders in Guilford were not committed by some random intruder from the world beyond but by the grandson of the couple.

Here Harvey pits the idea of place (as a secure bounded community) against what he calls the "uncontrolled vectors of spatiality." As is often the case in the history of geography, place stands against fluidity and flux which are portrayed as threatening. Note it is not Harvey who is saying that place can be a secure haven in an unpredictable world. He is simply observing that this is how the argument is constructed in the *Baltimore Sun*. Nonetheless his choice of this example does indicate something of the way he uses place in his own work.

> So what kind of place is Guilford? It has a name, a boundary, and distinctive social and physical qualities. It has achieved a certain kind of "permanence" in the midst of the fluxes and flows of urban life. Protection of this permanence has become a political-economic project not only for Guilford residents but also for a wide range of institutions in the city (government, the media, and finance in particular). And it has a discursive/symbolic meaning well beyond that of mere location, so that events that occur there have a particular significance, as signified by the response in the press and the media to the murders. Guilford plainly fits into cartographies of struggle, power, and discourse in Baltimore city in very special ways. But different maps locate it differently, as the two contrasting reports in the *Sun* clearly indicated. (Harvey 1996, 293)

Here Harvey uses the well-rehearsed and familiar characteristics of place ("a discursive/symbolic meaning well beyond that of mere location") to argue that it is just such characteristics that become important in the attempts of privileged groups in Baltimore to further "fix" Guilford as a secure white bourgeois place. It is important to bear in mind Harvey's choice of example when exploring the rest of his paper on the nature of place. One aspect of place that the example does clearly show (and this was Harvey's intention) is that places don't just exist but that they are always and continually being socially constructed by powerful institutional forces in society.

> Place, in whatever guise, is like space and time, a social construct. This is the baseline proposition from which I start. The only interesting question that can then be asked: is by what social process(es) is place constructed? There are two ways to get a fix on that problem. The first is to recapitulate what the relational view of space–time tells us:
>
>> entities achieve relative stability in both their bounding and their internal ordering of processes creating space, for a time. Such permanences come to occupy a piece of space in an exclusive way (for a time) and thereby define a place – their place – (for a time). The process of place formation is a process of carving out "permanences" from the flow of processes creating spatio-temporality. But the "permanences" – no matter how solid they may seem – are not eternal but always subject to time as "perpetual perishing." They are contingent on processes of creation, sustenance and dissolution. (Above, 261)
>
> A double meaning can, therefore, be given to place as (a) a mere position or location within a map of space–time constituted within some social process or (b) an entity or "permanence" occurring within and transformative of the construction of space–time…The difference in meanings is between putting down a marker such as 30.03°S and 51.10°W on a map of the globe or naming the city of Porto Alegre in the state of Rio Grande do Sul in Brazil. (Harvey 1996, 293–294)

So place, for Harvey, is a conditional form of "permanence" in the flow of space and time. Although using a completely different language, this recalls Tuan's observation that "if we think of space as that which allows movement, then place is pause; each pause in movement makes it possible for location to be transformed into place" (Tuan 1977, 6). But Harvey is more interested in the political world than Tuan, and the pause that comes with place allows not so much a sense of existential belonging but an opportunity to mark particular boundaries and constitute particular forms of local government and social power. Harvey's attention is focused on the "political economy of place construction under capitalism."

Capital is relatively free to move around the globe at the press of a button. Capital is mobile. Place, on the other hand, is fixed. This tension between mobile capital and fixed place is fundamental for Harvey. The "permanence" of place is a form of investment in fixity. Infrastructures have to be built that cannot readily be moved at a moment's notice.

> The tension between place-bound fixity and spatial mobility of capital erupts into generalized crisis, however, when the landscape shaped in relation to a certain phase of development (capitalist or pre-capitalist) becomes a barrier to further accumulation. The geographical configuration of places must then be reshaped around new transport and communications systems and physical infrastructures, new centers and styles of production and consumption, new agglomerations of labor power, and modified social infrastructures…Old places…have to be devalued, destroyed, and redeveloped while new places are created. The cathedral city becomes a heritage center, the mining community becomes a ghost town, the old industrial center is deindustrialized, speculative boom towns or gentrified neighborhoods arise on the frontier of capitalist development or out of the ashes of deindustrialized communities. (Harvey 1996, 296)

So the permanence of place and the mobility of capital are always in tension and places are constantly having to adapt to conditions beyond their boundaries. Places compete to get a share of the mobile capital – encouraging companies to invest in their particular form of fixity. Places have to sell themselves as good places to live and work and invest (Kearns and Philo 1993).

It is this mobility of capital that many see as the prime force of globalization and the main reason for the perceived homogenization of places around the world. As capital becomes more mobile and mass communication more ubiquitous, the argument goes, places become less important (Meyrowitz 1985). But Harvey resists this line of argument:

> But it does not mean that the meaning of place has changed in social life and in certain respects the effect has been to make place more rather than less important. This probably accounts for the vast outpouring of works over the past ten years or so in which "place" figures prominently in the title. (Harvey 1996, 297)

In conditions in which the global economy has reconfigured space and time radically, Harvey argues, people tend to think more about the security of their particular place in the world. The threat to place posed by the global economy makes us more aware of what we value in the places where we live and work. In addition the dramatic reduction in costs of transport and communication, at least in the developed world, has made objective location (how far a place is from other places) less relevant. This means that the qualitative aspects of place – the quality of life – have increased in importance when a multinational company (for instance) chooses a location. Thus:

> Those who reside in a place…become acutely aware that they are in competition with other places for highly mobile capital…Residents worry about what package they can offer which will bring development while satisfying their own wants and needs. People in places therefore try to differentiate their place from other places and become more competitive (and perhaps antagonistic and exclusionary with respect to each other) in order to capture or retain capital investment. Within this process, the selling of place, using all the artifices of advertising and image construction that can be mustered has become of considerable importance. (Harvey 1996, 298)

Think of the efforts of cities around the world to become "safe" and "attractive" places for people to live and work. So called "urban renaissance" projects such as the Guggenheim Museum in Bilbao, Spain, the Millennium Dome in London or the Portman Center in downtown Atlanta are part and parcel of the need to attract both businesses and consumers (i.e. residents) to particular places rather than others. Similarly large cultural events such as World's Fairs, Olympic Games, and World Cups are used to sell places to a world audience. Universities compete for students by advertising their location as well as their academic merit.

> Investment in consumption spectacles, the selling of images of places, competition over the definition of cultural and symbolic capital, the revival of vernacular traditions associated with places as a consumer attraction, all become conflated in inter-place competition. (Harvey 1996, 298)

Harvey's next move is to consider the formative influence of the work of Martin Heidegger and his notion of "dwelling." He notes (as Edward Relph had several decades earlier) that Heidegger sees place-as-dwelling as the "locale of the truth of being" – as the thing that makes humans human. He points out that Heidegger was already terrified of time–space compression in pre-war Germany because it resulted in a loss of place-based identity. It is this terror that forced Heidegger to withdraw from the world into his Black Forest farmhouse (see Chapter 2). Harvey finds this withdrawal problematic:

For example, what might the conditions of "dwelling" be in a highly indus-
trialized, modernist, and capitalist world? We cannot turn back to the Black
Forest farmhouse, but what is it that we might turn to? The issue of authenticity (rootedness) of the experience of place (and nature of place) is, for
example a difficult one. To begin with...the problem of authenticity is itself
peculiarly modern. Only as modern industrialization separates us from the
process of production and we encounter the environment as a finished commodity does it emerge. Being rooted in place, Tuan (1977, 198) argues, is a
different kind of experience from having and cultivating a sense of place. "A
truly rooted community may have shrines and monuments, but it is unlikely
to have museums and societies for the preservation of the past." The effort
to evoke a sense of place and of the past is now often deliberate and conscious. (Harvey 1996, 302)

Clearly, then, it is not possible for large numbers of modern dwellers to
retreat to farmhouses in the Black Forest or anywhere else (though where
I once lived, in West Wales, there is plenty of evidence of people moving
from the urban southeast of England to find some sense of attachment to
place). But all around us there are efforts under way to make places more
distinctive and visible and to provide a sense of pride and belonging. Often,
as Harvey notes, this takes the form of "heritage," where a sense of rootedness in the past and in place is provided for the consumption of locals and
tourists. Urban areas are cleaned up and marketed as heritage areas (I am
thinking of San Diego's Gaslamp Quarter, London's Covent Garden or
Boston's Faneuil Hall area). Signposts appear with elaborate "olde worlde"
maps and details of the history of this or that particular place. All of this
is part of a search for "authenticity" and rootedness. Ironically, of course,
they are only necessary because "being in place" cannot be taken for
granted.

But the new values put on place are not simply for the benefit of tourists.
Place has also become a political symbol for those who want to fight against
the ever-present power of global capitalism. As Harvey notes, Kirkpatrick
Sale was moved to write in *The Nation* that "The only political vision that
offers any hope of salvation is one based on an understanding of, a rootedness in, a deep commitment to, and a resacralization of place" (Harvey
1996, 302).

This permits a second cut at why place is becoming more rather than less
important in the contemporary world. What Heidegger holds out, and what
many subsequent writers have drawn from him, is the possibility of some

kind of resistance to or rejection of any simple capitalist (or modernist) logic of place construction. It would then follow that the increasing market penetration of technological rationality, of commodification and market values, and capital accumulation into social life...together with time–space compression, will provoke resistances that increasingly focus on alternative constructions of place...The search for an authentic sense of community and of an authentic relation to nature among many radical and ecological movements is the cutting edge of exactly such a sensibility. (Harvey 1996, 302)

This search for an authentic sense of place in the world is what Harvey (following Raymond Williams) calls "militant particularism." This term indicates the political use of the particularity of place as a form of resistance against the forces of global capitalism. All over the world groups have been, and are, attempting to build their own places and communities in order to live differently from the mass of people. Communes, organic farms, traveler communities, urban neighborhood groups, and religious enclaves are all examples of this. Also, Harvey continues, place is often seen as the "locus of collective memory" – a site where identity is created through the construction of memories linking a group of people into the past.

The preservation or construction of a sense of place is then an active moment in the passage from memory to hope, from past to future. And the reconstruction of places can reveal hidden memories that hold out the prospects for different futures. "Critical regionalism" as it is called in architecture, invoking as it so often does vernacular traditions and icons of place, is considered a basis for a politics of resistance to commodity flows and monetization. "Militant particularism" seizes upon the qualities of place, reanimates the bond between the environmental and the social, and seeks to bend the social processes constructing space–time to a radically different purpose. Some memories can be suppressed and others rescued from the shadows as identities shift and political trajectories into the future get redefined...Imagined places, the Utopian thoughts and desires of countless peoples, have consequently played a vital role in animating politics. (Harvey 1996, 306)

This construction of imagined places is important to Harvey (indeed he later wrote a whole book on the theme called *Spaces of Hope* (Harvey 2000)). It is in these imagined places (sometimes partly realized as utopian communities) that people act out resistance to the wider world of capital accumulation. It is not just small groups of people leading alternative lifestyles who use place to resist the forces of global capital though. Mainstream religions and nations also need to use place to emphasize what they see as their distinctiveness and independence from wider pressures. Thus nations invest in monuments, grand buildings, and other projects to fill the place of the nation with meaning and memory and thus secure their power and authority. In Britain the Labour government constructed the Millennium Dome in East London in order to produce a sense of national pride and project into the unknown future of the twenty-first century. In many respects this sense of investment in place shares much with the residents of Guilford seeking to protect and promote their little piece of Baltimore.

Harvey takes issue with the idea that a place can unproblematically stand for the memory and identity of a particular group of people. It may be true, he argues, that collective memory is often made concrete through the production of particular places but this production of memory in place is no more than an element in the perpetuation of a particular social order that seeks to inscribe some memories at the expense of others. Places do not come with some memories attached as if by nature but rather they are the "contested terrain of competing definitions" (Harvey 1996, 309). He uses the example of the Acropolis in Athens. While some argue that the monument stands for a particular kind of Greece that is unique and separate from the rest of the world, others insist that the place is the repository of a wider sense of "Western civilization."

> The burden that the Acropolis bears is that it simultaneously "belongs" to radically divergent imagined communities. And the question as to whom it "truly" belongs has no direct theoretical answer: it is determined through political contestation and struggle and, hence, is a relatively unstable determination. (Harvey 1996, 310)

In summary then, Harvey portrays place as a deeply ambiguous facet of modern and postmodern life. On the one hand, investments in place can play a role in resisting the global circulation of capital, but on the other it is often quite an exclusionary force in the world where groups of people define themselves against threatening others who are not included in the particular vision of place being enacted. The flows of globalization, on the other hand, are seen as anxiety-provoking for those people who seek to invest in the fixities of place-based existence.

Doreen Massey's paper is in many ways a response to this kind of thinking, a response that hinges on a redefinition of place as an inclusive and progressive site of social life. The following commentary refers to the paper as it appears in Massey's book, *Space, Place, and Gender* (1994).

"A Global Sense of Place"

Massey starts her paper by reflecting on the oft-repeated assertion that we live in a speeded-up and interconnected world marked by high levels of mobility which has created a level of uncertainty and anxiety in some quarters. This anxiety, the argument goes, leads some to retreat into reactionary versions of place. It is this view of place which her paper seeks to challenge.

But is that necessarily so? Can't we rethink our sense of place? Is it not possible for a sense of place to be progressive; not self-enclosing and defensive, but outward-looking? A sense of place which is adequate to this era of time–space compression? To begin with, there are some questions to be asked about time–space compression itself. Who is it that experiences it, and how? Do we all benefit from and suffer from it in the same way?

For instance, to what extent does the currently popular characterization of time–space compression represent very much a Western, colonizer's view? The sense of dislocation which some feel at the sight of a once well known local street now lined with a succession of cultural imports – the pizzeria, the kebab house, the branch of the middle-eastern bank – must have been felt for centuries, though from a very different point of view, by colonized peoples all over the world as they watched the importation, maybe even used, the products of, first, European colonization, maybe British (from new forms of transport to liver salts and custard powder), later US, as they learned to eat wheat instead of rice or corn, to drink Coca-Cola, just as today we try our enchiladas.

Moreover, as well as querying the ethnocentricity of the idea of time–space compression and its current acceleration, we also need to ask about its causes: what is it that determines our degrees of mobility, that influences the sense we have of space and place? Time–space compression refers to movement and communication across space, to the geographical stretching-out of social relations, and to our experience of all of this. The usual interpretation is that it results overwhelmingly from the actions of capital, and from its currently increasing internationalization. On this interpretation, then, it is time space and money which make the world go round, and us go round (or not) the world. It is capitalism and its developments which are argued to determine our understanding and our experience of space.

But surely this is insufficient. Among the many other things which clearly influence that experience, there are, for instance, "race" and gender. The degree to which we can move between countries, or walk about the streets at night, or venture out of hotels in foreign cities, is not just influenced by "capital." Survey after survey has shown how women's mobility, for instance, is restricted – in a thousand different ways, from physical violence to being ogled at or made to feel quite simply "out of place" – not by "capital" but by men... A simple resort to explanation in terms of "money" or "capital" alone could not begin to get to grips with the issue. The current speed-up may be strongly determined by economic forces, but it is not the economy alone which determines our experience of space and place. In other words, and put simply, there is a lot more determining how we experience space than what "capital" gets up to. (Massey 1994, 147–148)

Massey's first move in this paper is to question dominant assumptions about time–space compression and globalization. As we saw in Harvey's paper, these global flows of people, information, products, and capital are often seen as anxiety-provoking – as forces to be resisted. Massey's view is different. She argues that such views are the product of seeing global processes purely in terms of capitalism. And yet, she points out, they are also gendered and raced. The ubiquitous mobility of the world is too often portrayed as a universal condition resulting from transformations in capital. Harvey may agree that mobilities are often differentiated according to race and gender but these are not the aspects he emphasizes. Massey uses examples of people moving in all kinds of ways to show how the reasons for people's movements are far from homogeneous. Some are forced to move, some move at will, and others are effectively forced to stay still. To simply pit the apparent fixity of place against the apparent fluidity of the global economy, Massey suggests, is to miss the specificity of people's mobile experience.

> Imagine for a moment that you are on a satellite, further out and beyond all actual satellites; you can see "planet earth" from a distance and, unusually for someone with only peaceful intentions, you are equipped with the kind of technology which allows you to see the colours of people's eyes and the numbers on their numberplates. You can see all the movement and tune in to all the communication that is going on. Furthest out are the satellites, then aeroplanes, the long haul between London and Tokyo and the hop from San Salvador to Guatemala City. Some of this is people moving, some of it is physical trade, some is media broadcasting. There are faxes, e-mail, film-distribution networks, financial flows and transactions. Look in closer and there are ships and trains, steam trains slogging laboriously up hills somewhere in Asia. Look in closer still and there are lorries and cars and buses, and on down further, somewhere in sub-Saharan Africa, there's a woman – amongst many women – on foot, who still spends hours a day collecting water.

Now I want to make one simple point here, and that is about what one might call the *power-geometry* of it all; the power-geometry of time–space compression. For different social groups, and different individuals, are placed in very distinct ways in relation to these flows and interconnections. This point concerns not merely the issue of who moves and who doesn't, although that is an important element of it; it is also about power in relation *to* the flows and movement. Different social groups have distinct relationships to this anyway differentiated mobility: some people are more in charge of it than others; some initiate flows and movement, others don't; some are more on the receiving-end of it than others; some are effectively imprisoned by it.

In a sense at the end of all the spectra are those who are both doing the moving and the communicating and who are in some way in a position of control in relation to it – the jet-setters, the ones sending and receiving the faxes and the e-mail, holding the international conference calls, the ones distributing the films, controlling the news, organizing the investments and the international currency transactions. These are the groups who are really in a sense in charge of time–space compression, who can really use it and turn it to advantage, whose power and influence it very definitely increases. On its more prosaic fringes this group probably includes a fair number of Western academics and journalists – those, in other words, who write most about it.

But there are also groups who are also doing a lot of physical moving, but who are not "in charge" of the process in the same way at all. The refugees from El Salvador and Guatemala and the undocumented migrant workers from Michoacán in Mexico, crowding into Tijuana to make a perhaps fatal dash for it across the border into the US to grab a chance of a new life. Here the experience of movement, and indeed of a confusing plurality of cultures, is very different. And there are those from India, Pakistan, Bangladesh, the Caribbean, who come half way round the world only to get held up in an interrogation room at Heathrow. (Massey 1994, 148–149)

Massey gives many examples of people on the move which are easy to relate to and we can all think of others. Take, for example, the relationship between the global elite, the "ex-pats" for instance, who live in Hong Kong or Singapore, and the people who serve them – the domestic servants from the Philippines or the cleaners and maids who look after their rooms in Hyatts and Marriotts all over the world. They are all mobile but in very different ways and for different reasons. To think of them all as simply fragments of the globalization of capital misses the point. There are clear issues of gender and race in these examples too. Cleaners and maids in business class hotels in the developed West are usually poorer migrant women from the less-developed world. The people in the rooms are from different worlds. Hong Kong's ex-pat community is wealthy and predominantly white and male. The domestic servants are not. Massey uses the phrase "power-geometry" to describe the way in which the complicated movements of people are infused with power that is an issue not only of capital but also of other ubiquitous forms of social relation.

Massey's next move is to suggest that when we rethink "time–space compression" and "globalization" in these ways we also have to think again about place. She notes how one response to time–space compression has been the sense of anxiety that leads to people looking for a "little peace and quiet" and retreating into a romantic sense of place very much like the one outlined by Harvey. Such a retreat, Massey points out, is almost necessarily reactionary. She cites nationalisms, heritage crusades, and the fear of outsiders as examples of reactionary withdrawals into place. All of these were very apparent in the early 1990s when she was writing. Now we could think of the continued arguments over immigration quotas in the United Kingdom, the more generalized fear of the foreign in the post-9/11 USA and the treatment of Afghan potential immigrants to Australia as examples of the same kind of retreat.

Many of those who write about time–space compression emphasize the insecurity and unsettling impact of its effects, the feelings of vulnerability which it can produce. Some, therefore go on from this to argue that, in the middle of all this flux, people desperately need a bit of peace and quiet – and that a strong sense of place, of locality, can form one kind of refuge from the hubbub. So the search after the "real" meanings of place, the unearthing of heritages and so forth, is interpreted as being, in part, a response to desire for fixity and for security of identity in the middle of all the movement and change. A "sense of place," of rootedness, can provide – in this form and on this interpretation – stability and a source of unproblematic identity. In that guise, however, place and the spatially local are then rejected by many progressive people as almost necessarily reactionary. They are interpreted as an evasion; as a retreat from the (actually unavoidable) dynamic and change of "real life," which is what we must seize if we are to change things for the better. On this reading, place and locality are foci for a form of romanticized escapism from the real business of the world. While "time" is equated with movement and progress, "space/place" is equated with stasis and reaction.

There are some serious inadequacies in this argument. There is the question of why it is assumed that time–space compression will produce insecurity. There is the need to face up to – rather than simply deny – people's need for attachment of some sort, whether through place or anything else. None the less, it is certainly the case that there is indeed at the moment a recrudescence of some very problematic senses of place, from reactionary nationalisms, to competitive localisms, to introverted obsessions with "heritage." We need, therefore, to think through what might be an adequately progressive sense of place, one which would fit in with the current global-local times and the feelings and relations they give rise to, and, which would be useful in what are, after all, political struggles often inevitably based on place. The question is how to hold on to that notion of geographical difference, of uniqueness, even of rootedness if people want that, without it being reactionary.

There are a number of distinct ways in which the "reactionary" notion of place described above is problematic. One is the idea that places have single, essential, identities. Another is the idea that identity of place – the sense of place – is constructed out of an introverted, inward-looking history based on delving into the past for internalized origins, translating the name from the Domesday Book…A particular problem with this conception of place is that it seems to require the drawing of boundaries. Geographers have long been exercised by the problem of defining regions, and this question of "definition" has almost always been reduced to the issue of drawing lines around a place…But that kind of boundary around an area precisely distinguishes between an inside and an outside. It can so easily be yet another way of constructing a counterposition between "us" and "them."

And yet if one considers almost any real place, and certainly one not defined primarily by administrative or political boundaries, these supposed characteristics have little real purchase. (Massey 1994, 151–152)

To simply see place as a static and rooted reaction to a dynamic and mobile world holds several problems for Massey. First it may be the case that people do need some sense of place to hold on to – even a need for "rootedness" – and this need not be always reactionary. Second the flow and flux of global movement might not necessarily be anxiety-provoking. The reactionary sense of place that disturbs Harvey is, for Massey, marked by at least three interconnected ways of thinking:

1   a close connection between place and a singular form of identity
2   a desire to show how the place is authentically rooted in history
3   a need for a clear sense of boundaries around a place separating it from the world outside.

The first of these suggests that particular places have singular unitary identities – New York means this, Wales means that. Often these identities are based on ideas about race. Place at the national scale, for instance, often acts in a way that ties a particular "race" or ethnic group to a particular area of land. So the ex-British Prime Minister John Major famously argued that Britain was a nation of "long shadows on county cricket grounds, warm beer, invincible green suburbs, dog lovers and – as George Orwell said – 'old maids bicycling to Holy Communion through the morning mist.'" Clearly this is not everyone's view of Britain. The idea that particular groups of people with their own "culture" belong, as if by nature, in a particular place is, however, widespread. Successive American presidents have made similar statements about the United States. Ronald Reagan in September 1980 said in a televised debate:

> I have always believed that this land was placed here between the two great oceans by some divine plan. It was placed here to be found by a special kind of people – people who had a special love for freedom and who had the courage to uproot themselves and leave hearth and homeland and come to what in the beginning was the most undeveloped wilderness possible. We spoke a multitude of tongues – landed on this eastern shore and then went out over the mountains and the prairies and the deserts and the far Western mountains of the Pacific, building cities and towns and farms and schools and churches. (www.presidency.ucsb.edu/ws/?pid=29407)

Just as Major tapped into well-developed stereotypes about Britain as a particular kind of place, so Reagan mobilized long-held views of "America" as a frontier nation for particular political ends. There is almost a common-sense way in which particular identities are mapped onto the world. We will see in Chapter 5 how such visions often lead to reprehensible treatment of those who do not fit such an identity.

The second part of Massey's delineation of a reactionary sense of place is the constant desire to show how places and their identities are rooted in history. This explains the modern desire for heritage at both national and local scales. National governments and cultural elites are often keen to root a sense of national identity in a historical story about where it has come from and where it is going – a creation myth. Elaborate traditions are invented in order to bolster these stories. Museums display these histories. Not far from where I used to live and work in Wales there was a museum called Celtica which tapped into colorful myths about the Celts – the semi-mythical body of people who are supposed to provide the deep-rooted historical heritage of Wales (as well as Scotland, Ireland, Brittany, etc.). This is far from unique and places like it, can, I imagine, be found just about all over the globe. Often these histories are very selective and exclude the experiences of more recent arrivals. Returning to the idea of "Britishness," the Conservative politician Norman Tebbit made the following claim in September 2002: "My father's family came to Britain in the 16th Century, but I regard the Anglo-Saxon period, King Alfred and William the Conqueror as part of my inheritance." He went on to say how the challenge for modern Britain was, as he saw it, to "persuade these people [immigrants] that Waterloo, Trafalgar and the Battle of Britain, is part of their heritage" (http://news.bbc.co.uk/2/hi/uk_news/politics/1701843.stm). Here a particular exclusionary view of heritage is mapped onto a place – Britain – in a way that effectively excludes a large portion of the British population for whom other aspects of British history – colonialism, slavery, economic exploitation – may be more immediate.

Massey does not deny that there is an important connection between place and history. Such a view would be foolhardy. What she is arguing is that any place history is always also a history of journeys and connections. A local history is also a global history. Just as Casey has argued that places are sites where things are *gathered*, Massey argues for the "throwntogetherness" of place. Massey argues, in her book *For Space*, that places are gatherings of stories that make place specific.

> If space is rather a simultaneity of stories-so-far, then places are collection of those stories, articulations within the wider power-geometries of space. Their character will be a product of these intersections within that wider setting, and of what is made of them…And, too, of the non-meetings-up, the disconnections and the relations not established, the exclusions. All this contributes to the specificity of place. (Massey 2005, 130)

The third issue in the reactionary definition of place is that of boundaries. Boundaries are a key element in Massey's discussion. She makes it quite clear that, to her, places are not about boundaries. Boundaries, she argues, simply make distinctions between 'them" and "us" and therefore contribute to a reactionary politics. This, of course, stands in distinction to Harvey's tale of Guilford and the construction of very literal boundaries in the form of walls and gates around it. Of course some places have literal boundaries and others do not. Nation-states have boundaries which have to be negotiated. Political entities within nations also have formal boundaries that we often cross without noticing. On a smaller scale, however, we are often hard pressed to think of where a place begins and ends. And focusing on this issue, as Massey points out, tends to negate the multitude of flows that cross boundaries constantly. Massey's criticism here, however, is a little misplaced, as very few geographers (outside of those dealing with the geopolitics of national and sub-national boundaries) write about boundaries in relation to place. Humanists, for instance, would be the last to claim that place was clearly and unambiguously bounded.

Massey illustrates her points with reference to a main street in the North London suburb where she lives.

> Take, for instance, a walk down Kilburn High Road, my local shopping centre. It is a pretty ordinary place, north-west of the centre of London. Under the railway bridge the newspaper stand sells papers from every county of what my neighbours, many of whom come from there, still often call the Irish Free State. The postboxes down the High Road, and many an empty space of a wall, are adorned with the letters IRA. Other available spaces are plastered this week with posters for a special meeting in remembrance: Ten Years after the Hunger Strike. At the local theatre Eamon Morrissey has a one-man show; the National Club has the Wolfe Tones on, and at the Black Lion there's Finnegan's Wake. In two shops I notice this week's lottery ticket winners: in one the name is Teresa Gleeson, in the other, Chouman Hassan.
>
> Thread your way through the often almost stationary traffic diagonally across the road from the newsstand and there's a shop which as long as I can remember has displayed saris in the window. Four life-sized models of Indian women, and reams of cloth. On the door a notice announces a forthcoming concert at Wembley Arena: Anand Miland presents Rekha, live, with Aamir Khan, Salman Khan, Jahi Chawla and Ravenna Tandon. On another ad, for the end of the month, is written, "All Hindus are cordially invited." In another newsagents I chat with the man who keeps it, a Muslim unutterably depressed by events in the Gulf, silently chafing at having to sell the *Sun*. Overhead there is always at least one aeroplane – we seem to be on a flight path to Heathrow and by the time they're over Kilburn you can see them clearly enough to tell the airline and wonder as you struggle with your shopping where they're coming from. Below, the reason the traffic is snarled up (another odd effect of time–space compression!) is in part because this is one of the main entrances to and escape routes from London, the road to Staples Corner and the beginning of the M1 to "the North." (Massey 1994, 152–153)

Massey's description of Kilburn is a celebration of diversity and hybridity. Her portrait is an evocative mix of people of multiple ethnicities living and working side by side. The symbols she picks out are symbols of Irish,

Muslim, or Hindu life. This is quite clearly not a place seeking to distance itself from the wide world but one made up of constantly changing elements of that wider world. Massey's Kilburn is, in her words, a "meeting place" where a particular "constellation of social relations" comes together in place. It is a place she professes great affection for – but an affection based on its fluidity and diversity rather than a coherent sense of unitary identity. Massey goes on to more fully develop what this fluid, progressive sense of place looks like.

These arguments, then, highlight a number of ways in which a progressive concept of place might be developed. First of all, it is absolutely not static. If places can be conceptualized in terms of the social interactions which they tie together, then it is also the case that these interactions themselves are not motionless things, frozen in time. They are processes. One of the great one-liners of Marxist exchanges has for long been, "Ah, but capital is not a thing, it is a process." Perhaps this should be said also about places; that places are processes, too.

Second, places do not have to have boundaries in the sense of divisions which frame simple enclosures. "Boundaries" may of course be necessary, for the purposes of certain kinds of studies for instance, but they are not necessary for the conceptualization of a place itself. Definition in this sense does not have to be through simple counterposition to the outside; it can come, in part, precisely through the particularity of linkage *to* that "outside" which is therefore itself part of what constitutes the place. This helps get away from the common association between penetrability and vulnerability. For it is this kind of association which makes invasion by newcomers so threatening.

Third, clearly places do not have single, unique "identities"; they are full of internal conflicts. Just think, for instance, about London's Docklands, a place which is at the moment quite clearly *defined* by conflict: a conflict over what its past has been (the nature of its "heritage"), conflict over what should be its present development, conflict over what could be its future.

Fourth, and finally, none of this denies place nor the importance of the uniqueness of place. The specificity of place is continually reproduced, but it is not a specificity which results from some long, internalized history. There are a number of sources of this specificity – the uniqueness of place. There is the fact that the wider social relations in which places are set are them-selves geographically differentiated. Globalization (in the economy, or in culture, or in anything else) does not entail simply homogenization. On the contrary, the globalization of social relations is yet another source of (the reproduction of) geographical uneven development, and thus of the uniqueness of place. There is the specificity of place which derives from the fact that each place is the focus of a distinct *mixture* of wider and more local social relations. There is the fact that this very mixture together in one place may produce effects which would not have happened otherwise. And finally, all these relations interact with and take a further element of specificity from the accumulated history of a place, with that history itself imagined as the product of layer upon layer of different sets of linkages, both local and to the wider world. (Massey 1994, 155–156)

Massey's explorations of senses of place marked by flows and connections extend well beyond Kilburn and well beyond the human world. Since her original formulation of a "global sense of place," Massey has continued to work on this theme in intriguing ways. In one paper, for instance, she extends her analysis of a relational place to the world of physical geography. Observing the apparent permanence of a mountain such as Skiddaw, in England's Lake District, she reflects on how the rocks that make the mountain were formed many thousands of miles away and millions of years previously. Even something as apparently stable as the natural world is always moving and the landscape is thus made up of trajectories in ways that reflect the very different trajectories of Kilburn.

> Maybe instead of, or as well as, the time-embeddedness that enables that relational achievement of the establishment of a (provisional) ground, such histories push a need to rethink our security. Certainly such histories have the potential to be read as removing the absoluteness of such grounding, so that all we are left with is our interdependence, a kind of suspended, constantly-being-made interdependence, human and beyond human. (Massey 2006, 43)

To Massey, any place, whether the human/social landscape of Kilburn or the physical/natural landscape of the Lake District, is an event – a moment where things are "throwntogether." To Massey this necessitates a different ethical/political view of the world from that encouraged by thinking of places as separate and particular.

> Reconceptualising place in this way puts on the agenda a different set of political questions. There can be no assumption of pre-given coherence, or of community or collective identity. Rather the throwntogetherness of place demands negotiation. In sharp contrast to the view of place as settled and pre-given, with a coherence only to be disturbed by "external" forces, places

as presented here in a sense necessitate invention; they pose a challenge. They implicate us, perforce, in the lives of human others, and in our relations with nonhumans they ask how we shall respond to our temporary meeting-up with these particular rocks and stones and trees. They require that, in one way or another, we confront the challenge of the negotiation of multiplicity. The sheer fact of having to get on together; the fact that you cannot (even should you want to, and this itself should in no way be presumed) "purify" spaces/places. (Massey 2005, 141)

A "progressive sense of place" is "progressive" because it necessitates dealing with "throwntogetherness." The phenomenological attention to *gathering* in Heidegger via Casey, the notion of *assemblage* in DeLanda and the idea of weaving in Sack all point towards this throwntogetherness in slightly different registers. None of them, however, makes quite such a strong ethical/political argument as Massey does here.

Massey's observations of Kilburn and Skiddaw draw her toward a new "extrovert," "progressive," and "global" sense of place marked by the following:

1   place as process
2   place as defined by the outside
3   place as site of multiple identities and histories
4   a uniqueness of place defined by its interactions.

Massey's new definition of place is really quite different from ones that went before it. Tuan and Relph, you will recall, were quite clear that processes and forms of movement were, when extended too far, quite antithetical to the construction of places. The French anthropologist Marc Augé also sees travel as the moving force in the construction of non-place. So what would these writers on place make of Massey's use of the word? One criticism that it is possible to make of the "global sense of place" is that it is hard to point to anything specific about it. The traditional humanistic definition of place at least has the advantage of being quite clear about the importance of the existential sense of rootedness to make their arguments for the importance of place. What is the "place" component of Massey's Kilburn? Is it no more than an accidental coming together of many different flows in one location?

And surely it is also the case that many people all over the world do invest (in non-reactionary ways) in a search for comparative fixity. Although it is true that there are few places not influenced by global flows of commodities, ideas, and people, there are many places where families have lived for generations or where a little more globalization would be welcome. I am thinking here of towns where locals would like a branch of a global chain such as Starbucks, McDonald's, or Body Shop but the local economy is simply too marginal and depressed for these symbols of the globe to locate there. In Chapter 6 we will see how some groups make quite positive and inclusive attempts to tap into a place's history or promote a particular notion of place as an act of resistance and affirmation in the face of wider forces. In other words, a little bit of fixity might not always be such a bad thing.

A great deal, it seems to me, depends on what particular instance of place we chose to look at. Both Harvey and Massey choose to illustrate their ideas about place with reference to specific places near to where they live – Harvey writes about Guilford in Baltimore and Massey considers Kilburn in London (at least in the original formulation of a global sense of place). Both of these places obviously mean something to the authors personally. But notice how different the examples are. Harvey's Guilford is a place that sees itself under threat from difference and seeks to create clear boundaries – literally a wall with monitored gates – to distinguish itself from the threatening outside. Massey's Kilburn on the other hand is a place of radical openness, defined by its permeability. It is not surprising, therefore, that the more theoretical considerations of place that follow are different too. To Harvey place seems just too reactionary – too based on the exclusion of "others." Massey's Kilburn, on the other hand, allows her to suggest that it is okay to seek identity in place because the identity is never fixed and bounded.

Beyond Reactionary and Progressive Senses of Place

Stoke Newington is an area of inner North London which has been subject to gentrification. A new cultural elite has moved in along with their expensive and diverse restaurants, boutiques, and furniture shops.

> If we are to believe the pundits, Stoke Newington has arrived. Take a stroll through Church Street, the trendier of the area's two shopping centres, and the suspicion is confirmed. In place of the old barbers there is now a kite shop, instead of a butchers, a delicatessen. The fish and chip shop has long gone, replaced by a (reassuringly expensive) Indian restaurant and in its book

shops one no longer need to search through Frederick Forsyth to find the elusive little collection on Forster. (May 1996, 197)

Jon May conducted his doctoral research there and found that the politics of place in Stoke Newington should lead us to be careful about putting all our eggs in one theoretical basket in regards to place. His research involved ethnographic fieldwork and extensive interviewing of local residents – both working class and members of the new cultural elite. One couple, Paul and Pat, look back to the "good old days" of Stoke Newington as a cohesive working-class (and white) neighborhood where everyone knew each other and you didn't have to lock the door. For them the main reason the place has changed for the worse is immigration. They blame immigrants (i.e. non-white people) for crime and decay of community.

> JON: Because it must have been, when you were little, it must have been almost entirely white around here.
>
> PAT: Oh yeah, yeah! Yeah it was. And you left your front door open all night and it wouldn't matter. You know, it just wouldn't matter. But now! God, you got to lock everything up.
>
> (May 1996, 200)

To Pat and Paul, Stoke Newington is not a place of new and appealing diversity but a place in decline (Paul has suffered from a declining local job market and has had seven jobs in ten years – many part-time). Paul looks at the "diversity" of the area and sees scapegoats for his own precarious situation. Pat and Paul's sense of loss, although clearly racist, is nonetheless profound.

> Both Paul and Pat have seen the area where they grew up change beyond all recognition and such changes precipitate a very real sense of loss. For Pat, this sense of disenfranchisement has become centred upon the High Street where those landmarks through which she has always constructed her sense of place are being appropriated by others and where, when she feels as if she has nowhere to go, it seems as though others are being provided with a readymade sense of place. (May 1996, 201)

Despite the despair of Pat and Paul over the rising immigrant (principally Kurdish) population and diminished sense of Englishness, others are attracted to the area because it does "conjure up images of this England lost; a quieter more stable England of parish churches and village greens,

reaching back to the area's founding moment as the 'village in the woode'"
(May 1996, 202). The local council installed mock gaslamps along one
street while residents were busy installing wood floors and Aga cookers.
Two streets (Shakespeare Walk and Milton Grove) were granted conserva-
tion status in order to promote the heritage of the area. May interviewed a
graphic designer (Alex) who had recently moved into the area because of
the iconography of Englishness. Note how different Alex's perspective is
from Pat and Paul's:

> Coming from Church Street you've got that glorious shot of the church spires
> and trees and the park, and all that . . . it's a real sort of postcardy thing. The
> only that that's missing is the cricket pitch . . . It's very sort of Englishy, and I
> think it will probably remain so, you know. (Alex quoted in May 1996, 203)

So Alex sees Stoke Newington almost as a picture of stereotypical Englishness while Paul and Pat see only a lack of the very same qualities. Alex's
vision is similarly based on racial homogeneity. Neither of these visions of
the place could be said to be progressive. Both look to the past for a sense
of Englishness but they are very different visions. Paul and Pat look to a
past that is working class based on high street pubs and corner stores while
Alex buys into the (middle-class) iconography of churches and rurality.
This is best illustrated by their differing accounts of a local pub that had
been called the Red Lion and had been changed to the Magpie and Stump.
To Alex the change of name and the redecorated interior marked a distinct
improvement – it became a comfortable middle-class establishment that
Alex referred to as "traditional." Before the change the pub had been, in
Alex's eyes, "an awful place with about three people in there." To Paul,
however, this change was just another sign of the erosion of the place he
had known. The Red Lion had been a place Paul had grown up going to
and playing darts in. The Magpie and Stump was now a yuppie pub: "It
used to be a nice pub, and I mean the Red Lion, it's a nice name for a pub.
The Magpie and Stump! Why bring in the yuppy names, why not keep the
traditional thing?!" (May 1996, 203). As May puts it:

> Battles over an area's past are therefore of crucial importance in defining a
> local sense of place. But at issue is not some elusive question of historical
> authenticity, of whose image of the past is closer to what an area was "really
> like." Rather, it is a question of the material politics articulated by each vision.
> Ironically, that sense of Englishness – constructed through a particular
> reading of the area's past – that Stoke Newington's middle class residents are

building, is directly contributing to that sense of England lost that pervaded Paul and Pat's earlier accounts and complicating any ideas of a universal retreat into the mythology of a "bounded" sense of place. (May 1996, 205)

Beyond the senses of place of Pat and Paul, on the one hand, and Alex, on the other, May found another way of thinking about Stoke Newington that gestured toward Massey's global sense of place. Some residents were attracted to Stoke Newington because of its perceived diversity. Amanda is another resident of the area who takes pleasure in the sights and sounds of a local market place.

> It's just that I LEARN things there, I mean it's really humbling sometimes... for instance, there's a lot of Africans and West Indians that I talk to, colleagues and friends at work – more Africans – who really sneer at us because we are the so called "civilised society," but we've lost a big part of ourselves. Whether it's a spiritual part, or a bit that you can't really, you know, it's not logical, it's not material, and that's really quite recent for me. (Amanda in May 1996, 206)

To May, people such as Amanda enjoy a kind of aestheticized difference – they stand back from the crowd and enjoy it in all its variety. May argues that this is an appreciation of diversity as a picturesque scene that gives those who look on a sense of cultural capital – a sense of their own self-worth in being able to appreciate difference. For Amanda and others, "the city and its other residents are reduced to the sights of an afternoon stroll, part of an agreeable lifestyle aesthetic for those suitably insulated from the reality of life in a declining inner-city neighbourhood" (May 1996, 208).

Crucially this sense of an aesthetic appreciation of difference cannot be reconciled with either Harvey's or Massey's sense of place:

> [T]he images of Stoke Newington provided by some of the area's new cultural class residents suggest neither that radically "bounded" sense of place identified by some... nor yet the emergence of that more "progressive" sense of place championed by others... Rather, it has been suggested that we may need to recognize the multiple place identities people now draw upon and consider more carefully the ways in which such identities are constructed. The control over local space which Stoke Newington's new cultural class residents now enjoy, for example, allows such residents to construct Stoke Newington as a space in which "one can have it all." Whilst the neighbourhood's historical associations can support an image of place built around the

iconography of a mythical village England, those same residents demonstrate a desire for difference that draws them towards a more obviously "global sense of place." Yet the way in which this latter place identity is constructed is anything but progressive, suggesting we may need to pay more attention to the way in which such connections are imagined, and by whom, before automatically assuming that a global sense of place describes a more progressive identity politics. (May 1996, 210–211)

May's engagement with Stoke Newington and its residents provides a third example of the politics of place in a globalized world. Unlike the essays of Harvey and Massey, May's paper is based on several years of ethnographic fieldwork to find out the multiple ways in which people relate to the same place. Issues of boundaries and rootedness and connections are still there but they are used in complicated ways by people. The simple, observable, fact of diversity does not necessarily produce a progressive sense of place and the search for roots in history does not have to be reactionary.

Conclusions

These accounts of place, through the examples of Guilford, Kilburn, Skiddaw, and Stoke Newington, reveal just how complicated the idea of place is. It is not just that these are different places in the simple sense of being located in different parts of England or the United States. They all have complicated relationships both to the past and to other places near and far. These accounts also show how place is a way of understanding the world. The theorizations of place by Massey, Harvey, and May lead them to see different aspects of these places in the world. But theory is not just the property of intellectuals. Paul and Pat, Alex and Amanda, the residents of Stoke Newington, are also everyday theorists who bring their own ideas of place to bear on the place they live in. As with Massey, Harvey, and May they understand place differently.

References

Barnes, T. J. and Gregory, D. (1997) *Reading Human Geography: The Poetics and Politics of Inquiry*. London, Wiley.

Bird, J. (1993) *Mapping the Futures: Local Cultures, Global Change*. London and New York, Routledge.

Harvey, D. (1996) *Justice, Nature and the Geography of Difference*. Cambridge, Mass., Blackwell Publishers.

Harvey, D. (2000) *Spaces of Hope*. Berkeley, University of California Press.

Kearns, G. and Philo, C. (1993) *Selling Places: The City as Cultural Capital, Past and Present*. Oxford and New York, Pergamon Press.

Massey, D. (1994) *Space, Place, and Gender*. Cambridge: Polity Press; Minneapolis, University of Minnesota Press.

Massey, D. (2005) *For Space*. London, SAGE.

Massey, D. (2006) Landscape as a provocation: Reflections on moving mountains. *Journal of Material Culture* 11, 33–48.

May, J. (1996) Globalization and the politics of place: Place and identity in an inner London neighbourhood. *Transactions of the Institute of British Geographers* 21, 194–215.

Meyrowitz, J. (1985) *No Sense of Place: The Impact of Electronic Media on Social Behavior*. New York, Oxford University Press.

Newman, O. (1972) *Defensible Space: Crime Prevention through Urban Design*. New York: Macmillan.

Till, K. (1993) Neotraditional towns and urban villages: The cultural production of a geography of "otherness." *Environment and Planning D: Society and Space* 11, 709–732.

Tuan, Y.-F. (1977) *Space and Place: The Perspective of Experience*. Minneapolis, University of Minnesota Press.

5

Working with Place – Creating Places

So far this book has dealt with the conceptual problems of thinking about place in an interdisciplinary setting with an emphasis on human geography. Chapter 2 considered the history of the concept of place in philosophy and human geography while Chapter 3 looked at arguments about the relationship between place and mobility. Chapter 4 focused on debates about the nature of place in the face of globalization. This chapter and the next consider the way the concept of place has been, and can be, used in research and practice. Because place is such a broad concept, this is a potentially endless task. This chapter, however, considers work that uses place as an analytical concept in accounts of the process of shaping meaning and practice in material space. Research on place in this sense is necessarily concerned with how these meanings, practices, and material spaces are produced and consumed. With that in mind this chapter concentrates on a number of ways in which place is created. In the next chapter we will focus more on unexpected uses of place – practices that do not conform to expected meanings of place.

Thinking about and with place cannot easily be separated into "theory and practice." So although this chapter and the next are looking at the way place has been used in research and practice, that does not mean that they are not also about theoretical attitudes to place. The particular research and practical projects on place that people select are very dependent on what view of place they take at a theoretical level. These two chapters, then, provide an additional opportunity to revisit some of the debates in earlier chapters.

Place: An Introduction, Second Edition. Tim Cresswell.
© 2015 John Wiley & Sons, Ltd. Published 2015 by John Wiley & Sons, Ltd.

This chapter focuses on the various ways in which place is produced. But it is important to remember that places are not like shoes or automobiles – they do not come out of a factory as finished products. Places, as Pred, Massey, and others have reminded us in earlier chapters, are very much in process. Clearly places are created by cultural practices such as literature, film, and music, and the investigation of these forms of producing places are a central strand in contemporary human geography and beyond (Cresswell and Dixon 2002, Leyshon *et al.* 1998, Clarke 1997, Prieto 2013, Kreider 2014, Lukinbeal and Zimmermann 2008). But places are more often the product of everyday practices. Places are never finished, but are produced through the reiteration of practices – the repetition of seemingly mundane activities on a daily basis. As we have seen, the contemporary fascination with processes of flow and mobility in a globalized world often posits the end of place and the arrival of non-place. And yet place, even relatively fixed and bounded kinds of place, remains important. Small towns in Arkansas or even urban neighborhoods of London can be marked by considerable immobility. People are creating places at all scales and everywhere in myriad different ways.

This chapter is divided into seven sets of examples of ways in which the creation of place has been considered in recent research. The first concerns the continued importance of place in a mobile and globalized world at the scale of the room and the region, the second focuses on the production of places of memory, the third examines the ways in which place has been evoked in the work of architects, the fourth looks at the production of place-identities for places to live, the fifth considers the creation of place at the larger scales of the region and the nation-state, and the sixth section looks at the complicated layerings of digital technologies and place. Finally we encounter some of the ways artists have engaged with place.

Creating Place in a Mobile World

Geraldine Pratt, a Canadian geographer, explored the lives of Filipina contract workers in Vancouver. She tells the story of one woman called Mhay. Mhay used a room in the house of her employers to make herself visible.

> I bought a picture with a frame and put it on the wall. Prior to this, all four walls were bare. I did this without telling them because I thought that since I paid for this room, I should be allowed to do something about it. So I

arranged the room, put furniture and TV [the way I wanted them]. I would leave the door open so that they [my employers] could see what's in my room, that it's not dull anymore. (Quoted in Pratt 1999, 152)

Pratt pulls apart this observation in the context of feminist analysis of the notion of "home" and poststructural theorizations of hybrid identity. She traces the feminist critique of the cozy idea of home celebrated by Tuan in his notion of place as home. Home, as we have seen, has been the object of deep distrust by feminists such as Rose (1993) and de Lauretis (1990). The image of home as a peaceful and meaningful refuge has been described as masculinist – hiding the realities of power relations in the home which, at their extreme, are linked to battery and rape. In place of home some have argued that, in Massey's words, "One gender-disturbing message might be – in terms of both identity and space – keep moving!" (Massey 1994, 11). This is not Pratt's point though. She argues that it is much easier to make theory-level statements about home from the position of someone who has a secure one. Mhay, the Filipina domestic worker, in contrast, has a rather fragile claim to home as a domestic worker admitted into Canada on a special visa. Mhay lives a paradoxical existence of mobility and confinement with only the barest control over her own space – the little things that make space into place, such as a poster on a wall, get heightened significance. Pratt asks us to consider the role of place construction and boundary maintenance in the construction of identities.

> It seems to me that it is by starkly outlining the boundaries that separate my life from that of Mhay, by unravelling the layers of social–material borders that both produce and hem in our movements and identities, that a basis for communication and collaboration can be established. Marking boundaries, insisting on the materiality and persistence of differences, may be as politically productive as blurring them in notions of mobility, hybridity and third-space. (Pratt 1999, 164)

Pratt's observation is clearly a critique of the emphasis on the mobile and the hybrid in contemporary theory – pointing out that place and boundary still do matter even in the world of a migrant worker. Research on the place-making strategies of relatively powerless people at a micro-level is an effective use of the idea of place. Here Pratt's research with domestic workers raises some important questions about the kind of open and fluid place described and advocated by Massey.

The second example comes from the Colombian-American anthropologist Arturo Escobar. He is concerned with the hegemonic global currency of the term "globalization" and the way in which a focus on global processes in the realm of space can be brought into question by a renewed interest in place and the local.

> Subaltern strategies of localization still need to be seen in terms of place; places are surely connected and constructed yet those constructions entail boundaries, grounds, selective connection, interaction and positioning, and in some cases a renewal of history-making skills. (Escobar 2001, 169)

Just as Pratt was keen to show how Mhay was able to engage in place-construction in a context of relative powerlessness so Escobar argues that indigenous rainforest communities are able to construct places at a much larger scale. On one level this is a theoretical debate about the scale of enquiry necessary to understand power and the lifeworld. On another level it is a political project. In a world where forms of globalization associated with multinational flexible capitalism prevail and appear to flatten out difference – not least in the form of the development requirements of the World Bank and International Monetary Fund – maybe a renewed focus on place formation can provide a basis for subaltern strategies of "localization." Escobar shows how new social movements, particularly in Latin America, are "getting back into place." His examples revolve around the black communities of the Colombian Pacific rainforest. Activists of the Process of Black Communities (PCN) have articulated a complicated set of place-based identities in the face of the forces of globalization. Briefly put, strategies of globalization undertaken by the state, capital, and technoscience all attempt to negotiate the production of locality in a non-place-based way that induces increasingly delocalizing effects. In other words top-down globalization is insensitive to the specificity of place. Global capital does not care about the specificities of areas of the Colombian rainforest – or anywhere else for that matter. Meanwhile the strategies of localization undertaken by social movements rely on attachments to territory and culture and ecology. Simultaneously they activate global networks (in the United Nations for instance) around the issue of biodiversity which act to reaffirm the importance of local particularity. This is achieved through an emphasis on the uniqueness of local production systems in unique ecological zones geared to local markets rather than the demands of global capital. The production of a particular kind of nut which is unique to a particular place is one example. A key part of this is the construction of a "cultural ecology" of place. The region Escobar writes about is called the *Pacífico biogeográfico* and a large part of the place-making strategy used by activists rests on its unique biological resources. But the PCN cannot simply produce and defend place on this basis. Paradoxically, in order for localization to occur the place has to project itself onto the global scale of capital and modernity. This is not simply the substitution of place-based authenticity for global appropriation but a recognition that place can play a strategic role in a world of hypermobility. Theoretically, Escobar writes:

> It is important to learn to see place-based cultural, ecological, and economic practices as important sources of alternative visions and strategies for reconstructing local and regional worlds, no matter how produced by "the global" they might also be. Socially, it is necessary to think about the conditions that might make the defence of place – or, more precisely, of particular constructions of place and the reorganization of place this might entail – a realizable project. (Escobar 2001, 165–166)

Both Pratt and Escobar, through their very different examples, show how a new focus on place might simultaneously bring into question the widely held belief that places, boundaries, and rootedness are always necessarily either reactionary or a thing of the past. Pratt's domestic workers and Escobar's Colombian activists are both creating places from positions of comparative weakness in order to nullify the negative effects of globalization.

Place and Memory

We have already seen how an important part of the creation of a sense of place is a focus on particular and selective aspects of history. Notions of memory and heritage were right at the center of the debates in Chapter 4. Place and memory are, it seems, inevitably intertwined. Memory appears to be a personal thing – we remember some things and forget others. But memory is also social. Some memories are allowed to fade – are not given any kind of support. Other memories are promoted as standing for this and that. One of the primary ways in which memories are constituted is through the production of places. Monuments, museums, the preservation of particular buildings (and not others), plaques, inscriptions. and the promotion of whole urban neighborhoods as "heritage zones" are all examples of the placing of memory. The very materiality of a place means that memory is not abandoned to the vagaries of mental processes and is instead inscribed in the landscape – as public memory.

> If place does provide an overload of possible meanings for the researcher, it is place's very same assault on all ways of knowing (sight, sound, smell, touch and taste) that makes it powerful as a source of memory, as a weave where one strand ties in another. Place needs to be at the heart of urban landscape history, not on the margins. (Hayden 1995, 18)

It is, as historian Delores Hayden suggests, the very complicated nature of the experience of place that makes it an effective tool in the (re)production of memory. It is one thing to read about the past in the book or see it displayed in a painting – it is quite another to enter the realm of history-in-place. A similar point in made by Edward Casey when he writes of "place memory."

> It is the stabilizing persistence of place as a container of experiences that contributes so powerfully to its intrinsic memorability. An alert and alive memory connects spontaneously with place, finding in it features that favor and parallel its own activities. We might even say that memory is naturally place-oriented or at least place-supported. (Casey 1987, 186–187)

Recall that in New York's Lower East Side there is an area known as the Tenement District. It is here that poor immigrants often found their first home in one of the city's notorious tenements – buildings with very little light, packed with small living spaces often shared by large families. If you visit there now you will find the Lower East Side Tenement Museum – a preserved tenement with rooms arranged to demonstrate how they would have looked at different points in the building's history. It is an impressive place of memory because something of what it might have been like to live in these places is successfully recreated. The rooms are small, dark, and uncomfortable but full of items that were used over a hundred years earlier. Hayden reflects on just such an experience:

> In a typical New York tenement at the turn of the century, many people's sordid habitat was one landlord's money machine, generating 25 percent return on investment per year. There were few reasons to diminish profits through maintenance expenses, since legal enforcement of building codes and safety regulations was minimal. What did it mean in terms of the sensory

Figure 5.1 "Out of rear window tenement dwelling of Mr and Mrs Jacob Solomon, 133 Avenue D, New York City." Photo by Dorothea Lange. Source: Library of Congress, Prints & Photographs Division, FSA-OWI Collection [LC-USF34-009114-C DLC].

experience of place? The building will be a more evocative source than any written records. One can read about unhealthy living conditions, but standing inside a tenement apartment – perhaps 400 square feet of living space for an entire family, minimal plumbing, only one or two exterior windows – leaves a visitor gasping for air and looking for light. The claustrophobic experiences of immigrants living for decades in crowded, unhealthy space (as part of the reproduction of the labor force) are conveyed by the building in a way that a text or chart can never match. (Hayden 1995, 33–4)

This is what Casey means by place-memory – the ability of place to make the past come to life in the present and thus contribute to the production and reproduction of social memory. The Lower East Side Tenement

Museum is something of a rarity, however, in that it seeks to inscribe in place the memory of groups of people at the bottom of a social hierarchy. For the most part places of memory serve to commemorate the winners of history. Endless state capitols, museums, and public monuments in cities around the world make sure that a particular view of history is remembered – one of heroes on horseback. In many ways the Lower East Side Tenement Museum stands in contrast to a monument such as the Statue of Liberty which is often used to represent an official set of memories of the United States as a welcoming place for immigrants. Likewise the nearby Ellis Island Immigration Museum portrays a largely positive account of American immigration as a story of success and opportunity. It includes, for instance, a "wall of honor" on which people can pay $100 to have their immigrant ancestors inscribed on a wall. It is only recently that places have been designated as sites of memory for women, black people, the poor and dispossessed. Just as the inhabitants of a place like Guilford in Baltimore literally seek to exclude those beyond, so places of memory also enact an exclusion, literal and figurative, of those memories that are painful or shameful.

Andrew Charlesworth has examined the role of the Nazi concentration camp, Auschwitz, in Poland, as a place of memory (Charlesworth 1994). His paper focuses on the way the place and the memories associated with it have been contested. More specifically he argues that there has been a concerted attempt to "Catholicize" Auschwitz from the 1970s onwards – a process that has sought to exclude and marginalize specifically Jewish memories of the place as a site of genocide. Before and during World War II, at least 1.1 million people perished in Auschwitz. Of these victims, 87 percent were Jewish. A third of these were Polish Jews. Auschwitz was selected as a place of memory by the Soviet-backed communist regime in Poland following the war. It suited their purposes well as it could be portrayed solely as a symbol of fascist aggression. Jews from many nations had been killed there and this international aspect of the genocide meant that the government could effectively ignore the fact that the victims were Jewish and instead memorialize their international origins. The site became a place where Western aggression against the nations of Eastern Europe could be memorialized. Charlesworth described how official tours, publicity materials, an on-site film, and specific memorials always refer to the victims as "people" and "victims" and never as "Jews." In effect, this place of memory acted to de-Judaize the concentration camp.

Beginning in the 1970s, a Polish Catholic sentiment came to the fore at Auschwitz. Cardinal Karol Wojtyla, who was to become Pope John Paul II,

Figure 5.2 Christian cross at Auschwitz. Source: photo by Signalhead at en. wikipedia [CC-BY-SA-3.0 (http://creativecommons.org/licenses/by-sa/3.0) or GFDL (http://www.gnu.org/copyleft/fdl.html)], from Wikimedia Commons.

held several masses at the camp in which he mentioned a Catholic prisoner of Auschwitz, Father Kolbe, who had favored the conversion of the Jews. Father Kolbe was beatified. At one of these masses an altar featuring a huge cross was constructed at the very location where Jews were unloaded and sent to the gas chambers. Just as before, no specific reference to Jews who were killed at the site was made. In 1984 a convent was established at the site of Auschwitz and the contestation of the place of memory became world news as Rabbi Weiss protested the siting of the convent. There is also a church with a huge cross overlooking Auschwitz.

Clearly places have many memories and the question of which memories are promoted and which cease to be memories at all is a political question. Places become sites of contestation over which memories to evoke. Kenneth Foote, in his book *Shadowed Ground* (1997), suggests that places have the power to force hidden and painful memories to the fore through their material existence:

Figure 5.3   The Statue of Liberty, New York City. The Statue of Liberty is a world-recognized symbol of the United States which celebrates and memorializes a particular story of American nationhood as a nation of more or less welcome immigrants. It is an official place of memory. Source: photo by William Warby (originally posted to Flickr as Statue of Liberty) [CC-BY-2.0 (http://creative commons.org/licenses/by/2.0)], via Wikimedia Commons.

> As a geographer I could not help but notice that the sites themselves seemed to play an active role in their own interpretation. What I mean is that the evidence of violence left behind often pressures people, almost involuntarily, to begin debate over meaning. The sites stained by the blood of violence and covered by the ashes of tragedy, force people to face squarely the meaning of an event. The barbed wire and brick crematoria of the concentration camps cannot be ignored; they demand interpretation. A bare stretch of ground in Berlin, once the Reichssicherheitshauptamt, the headquarters of the Nazi state security, of Gestapo, compels the visitor to reflect on genocide in the twentieth century. (Foote 1997, 5–6)

The brutal fact of places such as these forces a debate about what they mean and what to do with them. People with differing interests have to make their case for preservation and what is to be included or excluded and thus

Figure 5.4 Ellis Island Immigration Museum hall. This room was used to process immigrants when Ellis Island was used as an immigration station. Now it is part of a museum built to commemorate the immigrant experience and its role in American life. Source: photo by Jean-Christophe BENOIST (Own work) [CC-BY-3.0 (http://creativecommons.org/licenses/by/3.0)], via Wikimedia Commons.

a new kind of place is born out of a contested process of interpretation. The connection between place and memory and the contested nature of this connection has been the object of considerable enquiry by geographers recently and promises to be a major component of geographical research in the future (Hoskins 2007, Till 2005, DeLyser 2005).

Gareth Hoskins, for instance, has examined the fate of Angel Island Immigration Station in San Francisco Bay (Hoskins 2004, 2007). Angel Island was the site of a series of buildings which were used to process Chinese immigrants as they entered the United States. Unlike Ellis Island, on the east coast, this site has not become a site of national memory and celebration of immigrant heritage. Rather it was forgotten and allowed to decay until a few local activists brought it to the attention of politicians and the public. The problem for those who sought to promote it as a place of heritage was that it was a site of deliberate exclusion under the Chinese Exclusion Act of 1882. This was the place where Chinese would-be immigrants were prevented from entering the United States and it does not, therefore, slip easily into a national mythology of inclusion in the "melting pot." Hoskins shows how the immigration station was developed by fitting into national-scale ideologies of belonging and celebration, thus obscuring some of the more particular narratives of exclusion and loathing. In order to obtain money and recognition, the station had to be reconfigured as part of a general national memory of immigrant belonging that hardly matches its original purpose. As Hoskins puts it:

> part of the price for official approval, national exposure and professional management expertise is that narratives conform more closely to popular and rousing patriotic notions of America where detainees become an object of veneration simply because they personify American ideals. In some cases this diverts attention away from the United States as perpetrator of the racism inscribed in the 1882 Exclusion Act and instead applauds immigrants' ability to overcome oppression at the country of origin by choosing to leave. (Hoskins 2004, 693)

Hoskins's explorations of the process by which Angel Island became an official place of memory carefully dissect the different ways in which aspects of place were mobilized in the production of particular memories. The materiality of the place – the things it is made up of – provides one set of cues for memory. The curators of the museum were careful in their selection of objects to include in the place – they were instrumental in the process of gathering that is so important to place. Hoskins shows how particular objects that appear in the Immigration Station museum are enrolled in order to produce memory effects. One of these objects is a bell that appears on the shore of the island overlooking the Berkeley hills across the bay. The bell is used as a gathering-point for the beginning of tours provided by docents that are constructed to imitate the movements of immigrants following disembarkation. The visitors are asked by the guide to imagine the bell ringing to warn nearby ships of the presence of land on a foggy day – and then to imagine the beginning of their detention in the station. Other, unofficial, stories proliferated about the bell ringing when an inmate escaped or to signal an arriving ship. One popular story suggested that the bell had been lost and was rediscovered in a San Diego junkyard. Such stories were untrue – but the presence of the bell in that particular place provided a foundation-point for such stories that became part of the memoryscape associated with the immigration station. The very materiality of the bell, as part of the wider place of Angel Island, enabled the evocation of particular "memories."

Figures 5.5 and 5.6 Ellis Island (above) and Angel Island (below). Unlike Ellis Island, Angel Island, in San Francisco Bay, has not become a nationally celebrated place of memory. While Ellis Island processed mainly European immigrants who have become part of the "melting pot" ideology of the nation, Angel Island was used to house Chinese would-be immigrants prevented from entering the nation. Source: Ellis Island photo by A. Coeffler, 24 February 1905, Library of Congress, via Wikimedia Commons. Angel Island photo by Hart Hyatt North *c.* 1943, The Bancroft Library, University of California, Berkeley.

> A focus on the material properties of the Immigration Station bell, for instance, suggests new ways to be sensitive to the many and often unexpected contributions brought about by the materiality of an object. The unexplained absence of the bell confounds conventional interpretation sparking off tales of mystery: its physical location at the beach in front of the site provides a place to begin the reworked official tour, its sound allows an evocative story of immigrant arrival, the characteristics of its hanging provoke photo opportunities, and its tactile functionality draws out the potential campanologist in many of the visitors. In each case, different aspects of the materiality of the bell are enlisted within social relations. Some are practices that the official park interpreters might well approve of, even work to instigate; others are met with consternation and are subject to alteration. (Hoskins 2007, 452–453)

Materiality is only one aspect of the production of a place of memory in Hoskins's account – it is always tied to narrative – to stories (stories told about and with the bell in this case) and practices (the act of ringing, the construction of tours led by docents). Materiality, meaning, and practice are combined in the production of a place of memory.

Place and Architecture

Architects design buildings. They also plan places. While this may seem obvious it has not always been clear to architects or theorists of architecture. Too often architecture seemed to be about buildings as discrete, disconnected entities with a set of functions and a façade rather than as key components in places. The fact that buildings are both places themselves and central parts of larger places has often escaped the discipline of architecture. Recently, however, both practicing architects and writers on architecture have recognized the importance of place in a number of disparate ways (Hornstein 2011, Norberg-Schulz 2000, Dovey 1999, 2010).

A recent retrospective of the work of star architect Richard Rogers, at the Royal Academy in London, painted his career as an engagement with the idea of place. Rogers, the exhibition blurb stated, believed that "a sense of place is what generates the character of architecture. Without this, buildings are generally banal" and that good architecture would produce " 'Open-minded' or multifunctional public spaces" that would "encourage interaction between diverse social groups. Encounters in which architecture plays a vital role" (Royal Academy of Arts 2013). Rogers is well known for his large projects such as the Pompidou Center in Paris and Terminal 5 at London's Heathrow Airport. To some, he (and "starchitects" like him) has been responsible for a proliferating number of mega-projects across the world that are part of the process by which places become less distinctive. Nevertheless, it is interesting that Rogers believes that his practice puts place at the center of things. It suggests, at the very least, that place has a particular salience that cannot be glossed over.

One key concept that has emerged from the discipline of architecture is *genius loci*. This term harks back to the Roman belief that places had a particular spirit that watched over them – a kind of guardian angel for a place rather than a person. The term gained particular prominence in eighteenth-century England when poets and landscape gardeners evoked a particular genius of place in advocating particular kinds of ordering in the landscape. Consider the following lines from Alexander Pope's poem, "Epistle IV, to Richard Boyle, Earl of Burlington":

> Consult the genius of the place in all;
> That tells the waters or to rise, or fall;
> Or helps th'ambitious hill the heav'ns to scale,
> Or scoops in circling theatres the vale;
> Calls in the country, catches opening glades,
> Joins willing woods, and varies shades from shades,
> Now breaks, or now directs, th'intending lines;
> Paints as you plant, and, as you work, designs.

Here Pope is urging landscape gardeners (a new profession in eighteenth-century England) to pay attention to the balance and composition of landscape in creating their gardens. The place is said to have a pre-existing sense to it that should be used in the production of the garden. The *genius loci* is both already there in the landscape and the potential product of judicious alterations. This is no longer an actual deity, as it was in Roman times, but more of a sense, or spirit, of place in the land itself.

In the modern West, the term *genius loci* has come to refer to a more general "spirit of place" – not far removed from the idea of "sense of place." The evolution of the term has been described by the landscape writer J. B. Jackson.

"Sense of place" is a much-used expression, chiefly by architects but taken over by urban planners and interior decorators and the promoters of condominiums, so that now it means very little. It is an awkward and ambiguous translation of the Latin term *genius loci*. In classical times it means not so much the place itself as the guardian divinity of that place…in the eighteenth century the Latin phrase was usually translated as "the genius of a place," meaning its influence. (Jackson 1994, 157)

The idea of *genius loci* has been developed most fully by Christian Norberg-Schulz in his attempt to develop a phenomenology of architecture (Norberg-Schulz 1980). Norberg-Schulz, both an architect and a theorist of architecture, uses *genius loci* to describe the assemblage of physical and symbolic values in the environment. In this reading, *genius loci* includes both "natural" aspects of a place, such as climate conditions and topography, and the human landscape. The architect has to read a place and then build in a way that is sensitive to the *genius loci*.

> To identify with a place primarily means to be open to its character or "genius loci" and to have a place in common means to share the experience of the local character. To respect the place, finally, means to adapt new buildings to this character. (Norberg-Schulz 1985, 63)

The architect, he argues, has to be able to read this accumulation of things to produce good architecture that fits into the *genius loci* of a particular place: "Architecture means to visualize the 'genius loci,' and the task of the architect is to create meaningful places, whereby he helps man to dwell" (Norberg-Schulz 1980, 5). The idea of *genius loci* has informed particularly conservative forms of architecture and town planning – such as the so-called "new urbanism" or "neotraditional architecture" – which seeks to replicate old or traditional styles of architecture in order to produce a new sense of place from scratch. Such attempts, it has been argued, might paradoxically lead to increasing "placelessness" and "inauthenticity" (Jiven and Larkham 2003). These are also not quite true to the definition of *genius loci* as discussed by Norberg-Shulz – "To respect the "genius loci" does not mean to copy old models. It means to determine the identity of the place and to interpret it in ever new ways" (Norberg-Schulz 1980, 182).

Norberg-Schulz is certainly not the only architectural theorist to focus on phenomenological approaches to place in writing and practice. One very influential writer is Christopher Alexander, whose book, *A Pattern Language* (written with Sara Ishikawa and Murray Silverstein), has influenced any number of attempts to produce holistic buildings that attempt to challenge modern approaches to architecture (Alexander *et al.* 1977). Alexander outlines a collection of patterns which can be used to build a human landscape that is holistic and life-affirming. These patterns range in scale from the corner of a room through neighborhoods and towns right up to the whole globe. It is a kind of recipe book for making a more wholesome and nurturing – more place-oriented – world. In the same book we find the suggestion that neighborhoods need clear boundaries to encourage community and the idea that uniform ceilings in buildings should be avoided and that varied ceiling heights encourage different levels of intimacy. Alexander believes that good architectural practice can be learned from existing places that work. These places are most often ones we might think of as "traditional." Alexander, in a later work, insisted that there is just one "timeless" way of building that is the right way to produce rich places (Alexander 1979). Not surprisingly, Alexander's idea have been enthusiastically taken up by the "New Urbanism" and advocates of neotraditional town planning (Duany *et al.* 2010). He has also been influential with architects who are seeking to think of buildings not as freestanding structures that could be anywhere but as holistic places that have the capacity to make us healthy or sick. Among these are the architect Christopher Day and the physician Esther Sternberg, both of whom argue that buildings as places can make us ill (sick-building syndrome) or play a role in healing (Day 1993, Sternberg 2009). As with Alexander, these authors ask architects to be attentive to the wider spirit of place when creating buildings so that they might deepen the aura of a place rather than dilute it.

The work of Norberg-Schulz, Alexander, and others insists on the close bond between buildings and the local sense of place. Architecture, for them, must be contextual. Kenneth Frampton, another architectural theorist, has similarly attempted to wed the practice of architecture to readings of place – but not in a way which seeks to reproduce a conservative sense of place. Frampton proposed a postmodern architectural practice he referred to as critical regionalism. Like Norberg-Schulz, Frampton argued for an architectural engagement with the natural resources of a place (region). He compared such an engagement with architecture which simply levels a site to produce an endlessly reproducible "modern" form of architecture: "The bulldozing of an irregular topography into a flat site is clearly a technocratic gesture which aspires to a condition of absolute placelessness, whereas the terracing of the same site to receive the stepped form of a building is an engagement in the act of 'cultivating' the site" (Frampton 1985, 86). He had no hesitation in advocating non-local materials and techniques when necessary. A critical regionalism would mediate between the local reading of place and elements of a universal civilization. He was concerned to avoid a romantic nostalgia for a place already lost. But he did advocate a careful reading of the land in a way that mobilized more than the sense of sight. Sight, he suggests, is part and parcel of Western universalizing tendencies and has often resulted in the denuding of richly multi-sensory places. He suggests that architects should produce "tactile" places and that the tactile is one tool in the struggle to "transcend the mere appearance of the technical in much the same way as the place-form has the potential to withstand the relentless onslaught of global modernization" (Frampton 1985, 29). Critical regionalism holds place as a central concept in the development of architecture that escapes being twee and nostalgic but contests the homogenizing forces of capitalist modernity.

At the other end of the spectrum of architectural theory and practice from Norberg-Schulz are those who advocate determinedly modern architecture. Place remains important, but only as a challenge to constructing buildings that are new. A prime example is the architect Bernard Tschumi. Tschumi starts from the proposition that architecture is focused on movement and eventfulness. It is the way that a building is used and moved through that defines it. This premise leads him to contrast a new architecture based on buildings and spaces as vectors rather than edifices rooted in a deep "sense of place." In one of his most famous projects, the Parc de la Villette in Paris, he superimposed a grid pattern on the topography of Paris. The park is full of walkways and linear shelters – spaces in which things might happen in unpreprogramed ways. Tschumi provides a provocative account of how the park worked not with, but against, the geography and history of the Paris neighborhood that surrounded it.

The grid, then, presented the project team with a series of dynamic oppositions. We had to design a park: the grid was antinature. We had to fulfill a number of functions: the grid was antifunctional. We had to be realists: the grid was abstract. We had to respect the local context: the grid was anticontextual. We had to be sensitive to site boundaries: the grid was infinite. We had to take into account political and economic indetermination: the grid

Figure 5.7 The inside of Nant-y-Cwm Steiner School in West Wales, designed by Christopher Day. Day believes in the necessity of building a holistic place that encourages well-being. Rounded corners are preferred to right angles, calming colors are used. Source: photo by Humphrey Bolton, http://www.geograph.org.uk/photo/603950. Creative CommonsAttribution-ShareAlike 2.0 Generic (CC BY-SA 2.0).

was determinate. We had to acknowledge garden precedents: the grid has no origin, it opened onto an endless recession into prior images and signs. (Tschumi 1994, 195)

Here Tschumi provides practically a mirror image of Alexander or Norberg-Schulz. While they look to a unique *genius loci* as an appropriate setting for building, Tschumi insists that his park refuses to be part of history ("garden precedents") or geography ("local context"). Despite the apparent radical difference between Norberg-Schulz and Tschumi they are both concerned with place – just different conceptions of what place is. While

Figure 5.8   Parc de la Villette, Paris, designed by Bernard Tschumi. Tschumi believed in radically departing from the historical context of the local area in designing this park. It is marked by modern abstract forms, straight lines, and right angles. Source: photo by Jean-Marie Hullot from France (Parc de la Villette Uploaded by paris 17) [CC-BY-SA-2.0 (http://creativecommons.org/licenses/by -sa/2.0)], via Wikimedia Commons.

Norberg-Schulz and others look for a particular, highly contextual spirit of place based on deep-rooted attachments, Tschumi starts from a belief that places are movement-based – that they are knots of vectors, velocities, and trajectories that make the world eventful and therefore interesting. While Norberg-Schulz's approach is more phenomenological (informed by Heidegger), Tschumi's is more poststructuralist (informed by Derrida and Deleuze). And neither of these are the same as the practice of Richard Rogers. It is unlikely that Norberg-Schulz or Christopher Day would recognize Heathrow's Terminal 5 as an exemplar of the "spirit of place" and yet Rogers believes that his architectural practice has the idea of place at its heart – an idea of place that emphasizes the coming together of diverse publics in an urban setting.

A Nice Place to Live

"Home" is a concept that reappears throughout this book. As an elementary and ideal (for some) form of place it lies right at the heart of human geography. It is for this reason that the idea of a student making university accommodation into "their place" was an early example of place in the introduction. Most people are familiar with the attempt to make somewhere feel like home. Even if there are many instances where they do not succeed, the attempt is important. The creation of "nice places to live" is one of the central ways in which places are produced. But take this activity beyond the seemingly innocent practices of decorating walls and arranging furniture and it soon becomes a political issue.

Let us return, once again, to New York's Lower East Side. As we have seen, by the 1980s the area was subject to gentrification – the purchase of run-down housing at cheap prices by middle-class incomers and the subsequent upgrading of the property and massive rise in property values – a process that meant that previous residents of the area could no longer afford to live there.

> Realtors, developers and gentrifiers portrayed as "urban cowboys" – rugged individualists, driven in pursuit of civic betterment – tame and reclaim the dilapidated communities of the downtown urban frontier. At their hands, city neighbourhoods are transformed as residences are rehabilitated and new luxury apartment complexes are constructed for incoming middle- and upper-class residents. New boutique landscapes of consumption emerge catering to their gastronomic, fashion and entertainment demands, and new landscapes of production are created with the construction of new office buildings: the workspace of the residents of the "new" city. (Reid and Smith 1993, 193)

Laura Reid and Neil Smith argue that this mythology of the frontier (a boundary where "savagery" meets "civilization") hides a process which is far from benign. Whereas city government and property entrepreneurs describe the process in the language of improvement (people returning to the city from the suburbs, historic buildings being refurbished, nicer restaurants, etc.) there are many people, poorer people, who are displaced as a new kind of place, a new kind of "home" is produced according to middle-class tastes and bank accounts. For a frontier to exist there have to be the two sides of savagery and civilization. In the Lower East Side the "working-class, poor, female-headed households and Latino/Latina and African-American 'natives' of the downtown neighbourhoods" (Reid and Smith 1993, 195) play the role of the "savage" in the face of the "civilization" of expensive loft apartments and cappuccino bars.

Reid and Smith describe the central importance of the arts industry, city government policy, and real estate speculation in the production of this frontier in the Lower East Side. They describe how the city's housing policy aimed to promote the gentrification process through the auctioning off of much of the city-owned housing which had been available for people who could not afford New York City rents. Part of the plan was to encourage artists by specifying particular properties for their use. They sought to play with the area's well-established reputation as a bohemian and avant-garde kind of place in order to boost the property prices by attracting in young urban professionals (yuppies) who enjoyed the idea of living a little bit dangerously in the city rather than the suburbs. Alongside this, the city government changed the way it policed and regulated public space in the area. So called "undesirables" were removed from parks and other public places. Prostitutes, drug-dealers, the homeless, and kids hanging out on street corners were cleared from the parks and streets to make the area a "nicer place to live" for the incoming gentrifiers. These processes were all met with resistance from local residents who were opposed to the gentrification processes. What created a nice "home" for the middle class was experienced as displacement by the poor. Protestors likened gentrification to "genocide" and "class war" rather than the taming of the frontier. They portrayed gentrification as an attack on their ways of life, their communities and their "home."

> Such an alternative scripting of the gentrification process aims at shattering the frontier myths constructed and purveyed by the media, the City and the real estate industry. Gentrification, they argue, is not for the good of all and is not a progressive development from the perspective of the community and its residents. For them, it means homelessness, displacement, expensive and inaccessible housing, and a challenge to the cultural diversity, practices and tolerance that have been a mark of their neighbourhood. (Reid and Smith 1993, 199)

Gentrifiers are not the only people with money looking for a "nice place to live." A relatively recent development in American town planning is the rise of so-called "neotraditionalism." Behind this movement is a desire to create places that are different from the anonymous sprawling suburbs of tract developments and "McMansions." Words such as "community" and "history" are often placed at the center of such attempts. The geographer Karen Till has looked at one such place – the urban village of Rancho Santa Margarita in Orange County in California. She argues that the place is created through the invention of traditions to "validate the establishment of a residential community by providing a sense of historical continuity and stability." They are, she continues, "created by corporate planners in order to give the place a sense of identity":

> These planners assert that, unlike their predecessors, they pay attention to the unique nature of places, to their local histories, architectures and urban and residential forms; and to traditional human–land relationships. They maintain that their towns and villages are "good places to live," places that can "revive public life," and return the "bonds of authentic community" to American society. (Till 1993, 710)

Note how the language that is used by the neotraditionalists reflects the more abstract musings on place by Heidegger, Relph, and others – place as an authentic form of dwelling rooted in history. Seemingly abstract and philosophical ideas are rarely confined to the pages of philosophers and theorists.

Till shows how the developers of Rancho Santa Margarita, a totally planned community, attempted to promote the idea of a place rooted in history through materials which focused on the themes of family history and early Californian Spanish colonial architecture. The landowners of the development made a lot of their family history, claiming that they were continuing the traditions of their pioneer forebears. They published so-called "historical newsletters" with articles about the O'Neills' role in history. The newsletters where made to look old by using tan pages and brown ink. Much was made of the family's generosity in providing land for good causes such as schools and parks.

In addition to the newsletters the promotional material for this new community focused on the "preservation" of early Californian Spanish colonial architecture which combined red clay tiled roofs, stucco walls, and rounded archways.

> The architecture of Rancho Santa Margarita goes back to this early [Californian] tradition. And beyond, when 18th Century Spanish missionaries built California's first churches, missions and monasteries. Today many of these architectural elements from the past are being preserved in the homes and

public buildings of Rancho Santa Margarita. (Santa Margarita Company, quoted by Till 1993, 715)

Till shows how the combination of the family history newsletters and the focus on architecture lock the place into a well-known history of pioneers moving west and settling to produce a distinctive American culture. It is very much the perspective of a white European land-owning elite peopled by rugged cowboys.

> [T]here is little room left for stories from the perspectives of other individuals, including those of women, children, and/or gays from various cultural, ethnic, and socioeconomic backgrounds...Thus, the promotion of a narrow perspective – one which attempts to silence alternative readings and interpretations of familiar texts and symbols – not only enhances the status of the corporate planners as the community "experts" who construct "good places to live," it also imparts social values. (Till 1993, 717–718)

Here the idea of an authentic place with an authentic past is being manufactured as an image for consumption. It is a form of marketing aimed at getting people to buy houses in Rancho Santa Margarita. The homes themselves, and their so-called "early Californian Spanish colonial" style is, as Till reports, a selective reproduction of upper-class nineteenth-century romantic visions of earlier missions. The actual buildings are mass-produced by large building companies.

Accompanying this production of a sense of history and authenticity is a process of exclusion based on the identification of a threatening "other" beyond the walls of the town. In the case of Rancho Santa Margarita the threatening "other" is Los Angeles.

> The historic small-town identity that planners would like to foster, however, makes sense only in relation to the place memory of Los Angeles. The success of the former – the small-town identity – depends upon the experience of the latter – present-day suburbs and cities. Both identities revolve around popular conceptions of current residential experiences in southern California, and both draw upon popularized "memories" of those experiences in the past, before it became "bad" and "dangerous." (Till 1993, 722)

As we have seen throughout this book, the construction of places is more often than not achieved through the exclusion of some "other" – a constitutive outside. Los Angeles, here, is a place of sin, of social upheaval and moral uncertainty – a dangerous place. It does not take much to see this as a place coding for social others – poor people, the homeless, black people.

In Till's paper then, we can see how a "good place to live" is constructed through the promotion of a particular exclusive history, a selective romanticized architectural vision and a differentiation of Rancho Santa Margarita from a dangerous and disorderly world outside. The example of American neotraditional town planning is not the only example of the attempt to produce a "good place to live."

In post-war Britain, politicians and planners were keen to move people out of crowded London and into a ring of "new towns" around the metropolis. One of these was and is Crawley. Crawley is not like Rancho Santa Margarita in that it was intended as a place for the "masses." New towns have been consistently ridiculed since they were introduced as soulless places full of mass-produced buildings – places that are neither the country nor the city. They are seen as failed places.

The photographer and ex-geography student Sam Appleby decided to explore Crawley armed, as he put it, with a "camera, memories and French theory" (Appleby 1990, 20). He notes how the new towns were part of an anti-urban ideology that stretches back to the nineteenth century. The idea of the new town was an outgrowth of the earlier "garden cities," such as Letchworth and Welwyn Garden City, which had been the result of the ideas of Ebenezer Howard. Howard had seen the miseries of crowded Victorian cities and the backwardness of the rural areas. His idea was to enact a marriage of the city and the country to produce a place with the best of the country and the best of the city combined.

Appleby traces the career of one man, John Goepel, a commissioner for the new town of Crawley, who was responsible for naming the streets of the town for much of its early history. Naming is one of the ways place is given meaning. Tuan has described the role of language in the making of place as a fundamental but neglected aspect of place construction – as important as the material process of building the landscape.

> A principal reason for the neglect of speech is that geographers and landscape historians (and, I believe, people in general) tend to see place almost exclusively as the result of the material transformation of nature. They can see farmers chopping down wood and putting up fences and they can see workers raising the roof beams. (Tuan 1991, 684)

Naming, in particular, can draw attention to places and locate them in wider cultural narratives.

> To call a feature in the landscape a "mount" is already to impart to it a certain character, but to call it "Mount Misery" is to significantly enhance its distinctiveness, making it stand out from other rises less imaginatively called....
>
> Naming is power – the creative power to call something into being, to render the invisible visible, to impart a certain character to things. (Tuan 1991, 688)

Goepel's naming of streets in Crawley reflects this sense of naming as power. Early on he began giving the streets names he believed reflected "Englishness." These could be historical references such as Fleming Way and Newton Road (named after British scientists) but more often they referred to elements of a supposed English "nature." Appleby's home area of Langley Green featured streets called Hare Lane, Nightingale Close, and Juniper Road. Other streets were named after figures in English art, such as Turner Walk and Constable Road. All of these sought to locate the new town in both English history and a sense of the countryside – as if they, themselves, were part of an unproblematic "nature." The ideological nature of this naming process became more apparent when Goepel lost the power to name and the left-wing town council made Crawley a "nuclear-free zone" and began to name streets after heroes of the labour and feminist movements (Pankhurst Court). Goepel believed that "socialist mythology" was quite inappropriate for street naming; "evidently only his own liberal/ conservative historicism was capable of providing natural and fitting themes" (Appleby 1990, 33).

Goepel's naming of streets fits squarely into the anti-urban ideas of the planning movement's founders. They seek to link the brand new places into both a sense of history and an identity symbolized by the English countryside. This mirrors the use of family history and architectural styles in Rancho Santa Margarita. In both places the planners are producing their favored sense of place through attempts to connect the material structure of the two towns into well-known mythological histories – the story of the frontier in Rancho Santa Margarita and the nationalist anti-urban mythology in Crawley. Both these stories also seek to create particular place-memories in brand new residential neighborhoods. In this sense these examples are further evidence of the importance of memory and heritage in the production of place.

Regions and Nations as Places

For the most part geographers' use of place has reflected the common-sense notion of places as being relatively knowable and small scale – cities, towns, neighborhoods. But, as Tuan has suggested, the idea of place connects the favorite armchair to the globe. So how have scholars considered these larger scale places, the region and the nation? Political geographers have a long tradition of using the concept of place in their research. Notably, they have thought about traditional political divisions in space as having place qualities. The political geographer Peter Taylor notes how writers such as John Agnew and Ron Johnston have utilized place in their work (Taylor 1999). Johnston has written, for instance, about the resistance of Nottinghamshire coal-miners to calls for national strikes. He argues that there are specific qualities of Nottinghamshire as a place that made it likely that the miners there would go their own way. Places, in other words, have specific political cultures that trump national and individual arenas (Johnston 1991). Taylor considers the role of space and place in the politics of the modern nation. Nations, he argues, might easily be seen as political impositions of rational and abstract space over the specificities of place. But this argument, he suggests, is too simple and place, too, plays a role in the production of the nation.

> Nations have been constructed as imagined communities each with their own place in the world, their own homeland, some as "fatherland," others as "motherland." By combining state and nation in nation-state, sovereign territory has been merged with sacred homeland to convert a space into a place. (Taylor 1999, 102)

A nation-state is a curious thing. While they seem as natural as the air we breathe in the early twenty-first century they are relatively recent creations (for the most part of the nineteenth century). A nation-state, as Taylor suggests, combines the abstraction of space with the deeply felt emotions of place. How is it that a black inner-city resident of the Bronx feels they belong to the same community as the white businessman in Westchester County and the Mexican immigrant in San Diego? So much so that, when push comes to shove, many will fight for this thing called the United States. Theorists of the nation suggest that this is because the creation of the nation involves the creation of "imagined communities" where people with nothing in common in their everyday lives believe themselves to be connected through the idea of a nation as place (Anderson 1991, Edensor 2002). With this place, of course, comes all the paraphernalia of national ideology and belonging – flags, anthems, passports, money, and more. For a nation to hold its inhabitants together it must act as place – a field of care.

But within the place of the nation there exist other political units loosely referred to as "regions." These places sit, broadly speaking, somewhere between the scale of the nation and the scale of the local. Often the terms region and place are used interchangeably though region does not come with all the philosophical baggage of place (Paasi 2002). Just as politicians have sought to create a national sense of place so local politicians have sought to make politically constituted regions more "place-like." While political identity is most often conceived of within the scale of the nation-state: "sense of place at the national scale can coexist with or be replaced by alternative ones" (Agnew 2002, 6). Politics happens in local and regional places.

In Britain, over the past several decades, there has been a multitude of calls for "devolution" – the localizing of power into more immediate and small-scale "places." Wales and Scotland have succeeded in constructing various kinds of regional government. As I write, the citizens of Scotland are deciding whether or not they want to be an independent country. There is often talk of further devolution of powers to areas of England such as Cornwall or the North-East. More dramatically, regions of Italy have sought to promote their own political agendas over and above those of the nation-state (Agnew 2002, Giordano 2000). Benito Giordano has provided an account of the claims of Italy's Northern League (Lega Nord), a right-wing political party that claims that the Italian state does not serve the people of the North of Italy and is, in effect, in the hands of those in the South. Anti-Southern sentiment is a strong element in their success. As with many forms of place, the place of the "North" is constructed in relation to its other – the "South." Giordano interviews a Northern League councilor:

> The mentality of the people of the North is distinct to that of the South. In the North there is a strong work ethic which could be described as almost Calvinistic in nature. In spite of the high levels of taxation and the burden of the South, Lombardy is still one of the wealthiest regions within the European Union (EU). However, the South of Italy has a "Mediterranean" work ethic, which is based on corruption, a reliance of state transfers and a more relaxed attitude towards work. (Quoted in Giordano 2000, 459)

gender identities, suggesting both that gender identities were being challenged offline as well as online, and that the online world interacts with the actual places where the Internet is performed – such as a cybercafé.

Regardless of its clear intention to question the boundary that separated online and offline worlds, Wakeford's paper nonetheless reproduces the idea that there are separate worlds which are capable of interacting with each other. Since 1999 a lot has happened in the world of online technologies. Of particular note is the advent of GPS-capable mobile devices and the increased geocoding of information. Whereas cyberspace has previously been imagined as a separate, non-material realm – a kind of alternative reality – virtual worlds are now increasingly layered on to "real" places. Indeed – they are part of real places. Places have become "layered" and "augmented." Apps such as Foursquare depend on the people who use it "logging in" at favorite libraries, shops, cafés, or restaurants. Other apps tell you about local history and show you images of the place you are in from a hundred years earlier. You can find out which of your friends are nearest to you and then meet them for a drink. Many of the ways in which we now interact with virtual worlds are totally enmeshed with our use of the familiar landscapes of "bricks and mortar." Indeed, it is not just our GPS-enabled mobile devices that are linking bricks and mortar to virtual worlds; the bricks and mortar themselves are being "augmented" with all manner of devices that make the world increasingly interactive in new ways.

RFID (radio frequency identification) chips, for instance, are digital chips that cost around one cent each. They are attached to products so they can be tracked through chains of distribution. You might be familiar with them from their presence in library books. If you leave the library without checking out you will be detected. RFID works by communicating with detectors embedded in architecture. This is just one way in which our material environments include built-in digital technologies which correspond with our mobile devices.

One of the key writers on the augmentation of place is the architectural theorist, Malcolm McCullough (2004, 2006). McCullough has been tracing the rise of locative media and associated attitudes to place. "Whether the word 'media,'" he writes, "implies passive entertainment, global networking, production software, or the attention economy of all of these, it does tend to imply disembodiment; and that implies trouble for space and place as we know them" (McCullough 2006, 26). This trouble, he continues, has been made more complicated and somewhat ameliorated by the increasingly geo-spatial nature of most online information. We now live in a world, he argues, where the term "cyberspace" sounds distinctly retro. Information in the current digital age is likely to be about where you are and perhaps even specific to where you are.

> Perceptions of place may be subjective and fleeting, but grounding life in effective contexts remains absolutely necessary. Resorting to nostalgia hardly helps in doing this, however; there is little to be gained from understanding place mainly as something lost.
>
> At least to the more mobile and networked of us, place has become less about our origins on some singular piece of blood soil, and more about forming connections with the many sites of our lives. Place becomes less an absolute location fraught with tribal bonds or nostalgia, and more a relative state of mind that one gets into by playing one's boundaries and networks. We belong to several places and communities, partially by degree, and in ways that are mediated. (McCullough 2006, 29)

McCullough is also careful to put the rise of locative technology into a historical continuum rather than suggesting it represents a radical break. Both the place-based apps on our phones and the architecture of the city are, he argues, varieties of "technologies of attention."

> Many sites of life – kitchens, classrooms, boardrooms, laboratories, lobbies, sidewalk cafés, public plazas – are not only for particular activities but also about them. Sites put people into frames of mind, and often into particular spatial relationships as well, often at a very carefully considered scale. So in a way, you could say that architecture and the city have always been technologies of attention. (McCullough 2012, 41–42).

The geocoded information that can come to us through our mobile devices thus layers or augments place that already has layers of buildings, billboards, signs of a thousand kinds. Locative media thus represent part of an urban continuum rather than a new form of media that threatens to undo previous layers of place.

There are other continuities between place as conventionally understood and aspects of augmented place. The architecture, signage, and layout of a city neighborhood, for instance, are arranged in ways that direct our attention and compete for prominence. Some stories are made prominent (through a skyscraper or a cathedral for instance) while others you have to scrape and dig to find. The same is true for "DigiPlace." The word "DigiPlace" has been coined by the geographers Mark Graham and Matthew

Zook to refer to this "platial" aspect of the digital world (Zook and Graham 2007a, 2007b). DigiPlace refers to "the use of information ranked and mapped in cyberspace to navigate and understand physical places" (Zook and Graham 2007b, 466). The concept of DigiPlace is informed by earlier discussions of places as social constructs. Now, however, the process of social construction is complicated by the layering or augmenting of places with digital information.

> Moreover, it provides a focus on the ways in which the physical, tangible world combines with virtually accessible information and creates not a fixed setting for interaction, but a lived, fluid, and subjective space, shaped by space, time, and information. In other words, DigiPlace represents the simultaneous interaction with software (interaction) and "hard-where" (place) by an individual Thus, DigiPlace is the understanding of a location based on and filtered through information about a place that is available in cyberspace. (Zook and Graham 2007b, 468)

Zook and Graham explore the DigiPlaces constructed through Google Maps – one of the most widely used apps for gathering geographical information and navigating places. They place the process of constructing Digi-Places in the literature on critical cartography which argues that maps appear to be innocent and objective representations of the world, but are in fact highly pre-sorted selections of information (Harley 1989). Google famously provides responses to searches in pages that are ranked. Few people get past the first two or three pages of a Google search. This is referred to as the PageRank system. This system, Zook and Graham argue, is a highly opaque actor in the production of place when it is linked to geographical data in Google Maps.

> PageRank is problematic since it invites one to consider it a "natural" outcome rather than the result of specific human-designed algorithms embedded in software. These algorithms, however, are far from natural and are constructed with specific intents and outcomes in mind, such as the desire to circumvent would-be manipulators and the pressure to generate corporate profit. (Zook and Graham 2007b, 470)

DigiPlace, as experienced through Google Maps, then, replicates the way in which the landscape directs our attention in socially coded ways. In many ways, however, DigiPlace is even better at doing this.

In real space…filtering is usually imperfect. However much I'd like to ignore homelessness, I cannot go to my bank without confronting homeless people on the streets…All sorts of issues I'd rather not think about force themselves on me. They demand my attention in real space, regardless of my filtering choices. (Lessig quoted in Zook and Graham 2007b, 471)

Zook and Graham perform a number of searches on Google Maps for things such as restaurants and alcohol treatment centers. They use places they know well. In general they find that institutions with large corporate presences feature higher up the list, regardless of distance from the location of the searcher. Local businesses and services are often demoted or invisible – even when they are closer and more convenient. Thus invisibility in software is reflected in invisibility in place.

We have clearly come a long way since the early versions of virtual geography as alternative worlds that exist in parallel to the "real" one. The disembodied and disconnected world of cyberspace on the computer screen is now supplemented by the messier and more place-based world of media which are site-specific and full of place-based content. Through these technologies and software programs, places are continuously being augmented and layered with new sets of information which we can act on. The influence of communications technology on sense of place in the twenty-first century is a key research agenda across and between disciplines.

Place and Art

Early in 2008 it was announced that a huge work of public art – "The Angel of the South" or Ebbsfleet Landmark – had been commissioned to be built overlooking the Ebbsfleet transport terminal in Kent, to the east of London. The title, "Angel of the South," evokes artist Anthony Gormley's well-known statue, "Angel of the North," at Gateshead in the Northeast of England.

The call for proposals for the new southern statue stipulated that it must be at least twice as high as its northern equivalent. Ebbsfleet is part of the area known as the Thames Gateway, an area to the east of London that has become an entry point to the city for the Eurostar high-speed train link from Paris and Brussels. It is also a site for a planned new town to be built on green principles. This part of Kent is an area of high transience, marked by historically migrant populations, from hop-pickers to recent immigrants. So why build such an enormous work of art at this place?

Figure 5.9 The Angel of the North. Source: photo by The Halo (taken by The Halo) [Public domain], via Wikimedia Commons.

Rachel Cook, a journalist for *The Observer*, provides one answer (Cook 2008). She suggests that it is an act of place definition – a way of saying that this place is different and special. She compares the construction of such a work of public art to the act of shopping, in what she sees as the increasingly homogeneous retail landscape represented by Ebbsfleet's Bluewater Shopping Centre.

> In a way, of course, this is how we define ourselves: everyone knows what volumes a sofa speaks of its owner, what subtle hints the cut of a suit can drop. But, as a theory, it is also riddled with holes. For one thing, even the most dedicated shopper cannot distinguish himself in a world of chain stores. For another, for all that urban Britain increasingly looks the same wherever you go, this is just a surface. Behind its Ikea blinds, a place still has a pulse, a beating heart, even if listening to it grows trickier by the hour. (Cook 2008, 13)

Cook suggests that while shopping smothers the life of place by making things more and more alike, public art can bring it back to life – to make a place distinctive.

> This is when public art comes into its own. The best isn't just beautiful or moving in its own right; as we are fast learning, it can tell a story about a place, capture its visceral essence, in a way that the ad men – "Visit sunny Harlow!" – can only dream of. This is what the Angel does, and the people of Ebbsfleet will be hoping that their sculpture will pull off a similar trick. (Cook 2008, 13)

To Cook, then, art could play a powerful role in the creation of place. Art, however, has an uneasy relationship to place. Traditionally, up until the end of the 1960s at least, art was interpreted as though it were an autonomous thing with its own internal rules. Since then, some art critics, scholars, and the artists themselves have included the relationship between art and its place as part of both the production of work and the interpretation of it. One aesthetic strategy for artists has been "site-specificity" – a strategy that includes the relationship between art and place within it. The word "site" is a little misleading here as it seems to imply merely "location." What we are really talking about, however, is place – location plus meaning plus power – including what people do in a particular place as much as its materiality. Site-specific art frequently seeks to ask questions of the way an artistic object is made meaningful through its relationships to place and all the institutional frames that a particular place implies (Deutsche 1988, Kwon 2002, Suderburg 2000, Doherty 2004).

Site-specific art, however, is not the only way in which art is related to place. The practice and theory of art have often confronted the idea of place (Hawkins 2013). The art/place nexus happens in many ways. There is, for instance, an art of place where art attempts to represent place. The most obvious examples of this are paintings or drawings which are of a particular place: landscape paintings for instance. Think of John Constable's portrayal of Suffolk, UK (that has since become "Constable Country") or Cézanne's paintings of Provence, France. Beyond that there is the issue of the place in which art exists. We have an association of art with the particular kinds of places we call galleries and museums. That is where we might go to encounter art. These are places that have been set up as special, divided from the humdrum non-art world beyond.

The seemingly benign architectural features of a gallery/museum, in other words, were deemed to be coded mechanisms that actively disassociate the space of art from the outer world, furthering the institution's idealist imperative of rendering itself and its hiearchization of values "objective," "disinterested," and "true." (Kwon 1997, 88)

Some art seeks to question the place of the gallery either by asking questions of them or by being placed elsewhere – outside and in public. And then there is art which takes place as its subject matter at a more conceptual level – art which attempts to create a place in and of itself.

One (in)famous encounter between art and the gallery space was enacted by the artist Marcel Duchamp. In 1917 Duchamp took a men's urinal, placed it on its back and signed it "R Mutt." He entered his work, titled "Fountain," for a prestigious art exhibition. The contribution was roundly rejected as not art by the committee responsible for the exhibition – a committee which included Duchamp himself. He promptly resigned. Now, however, a number of versions of Duchamp's fountain can be found in the world's leading museums of contemporary art. Sometimes the questions art can ask of the place of the gallery are not intentional.

Another artwork that asked questions of the space of the gallery was "Equivalent VIII" by Carl Andre. Andre's work was bought by the Tate Gallery in London in 1971 and featured in several exhibitions without much comment before a 1976 article in the *Sunday Times* mentioned the art work – a pile of 120 fire bricks arranged as a rectangle – and uproar ensued. Along with the uproar came large numbers of viewers keen to experience the bricks for themselves. A good deal of the discussion surrounding the bricks was the role of the gallery in making something into art. Both "Fountain" and "Equivalent VIII" ask questions about what counts as art – but also about where something might count as art. The urinal in the hardware shop would not be thought of as art while the urinal in the art gallery, appropriately signed, might be thought of as art. A pile of bricks in a building site was not art while an equivalent pile in the Tate Gallery clearly was. The place of the gallery has the ability to make something more likely to be considered art.

A different set of relationships between art and place are revealed by work that clearly is art being sited in places outside of the gallery of the museum. In the world of art-practice the word "site" is most often used as a stand-in for place. Art is said to be "site-specific" if the place of its display is part of the point of the art piece. While a Constable painting relates to an area of Suffolk in the East of England by being a painting of a patch of Suffolk, there is no interaction between the completed art work and the wall it is hung on, in the National Gallery in London for instance. It is not a commentary on the National Gallery and neither does its meaning derive much from being hung there. It certainly gathers prestige as part of an artistic canon from being in the place it is in (and that is an important function of galleries as place) but this is nothing to do with the intentions of the artist. A site-specific work of art, on the other hand, often has to be in exactly the place it was intended for. This relationship between art and place can take several forms. One strategy is to produce a work of art that fits into a particular place – that is specially designed to belong. Another strategy is to produce art that has a more critical and interrogative mode – art that questions and critiques the site it is in.

The art-writer, Miwon Kwon, has proposed three paradigms of site-specific art: phenomenological/experiential, social/institutional, and discursive (Kwon 1997). The first of these resonates with the concerns of humanistic geography. It suggests a tight connection between the work of art and the place where it belongs (much in the same way as a person can be said to belong).

> The space of art was no longer perceived as a blank slate, a tabula rasa, but a real place. The art object or event in this context was to be singularly experienced in the here-and-now through the bodily experience of each viewing subject, in a sensorial immediacy or spatial extension and temporal duration…rather than instantaneously "perceived" in a visual epiphany by a disembodied eye. (Kwon 1997, 86)

The relationship between the place and the work of art is said to be authentic or organic. Kwon's second paradigm – the social/institutional paradigm – moves away from seemingly organic senses of place and, instead, constantly seeks to undo the supposition that there is any such thing as organic or authentic place/site. If the phenomenological/experiential paradigm mapped on to the concerns of humanistic geography then the social/institutional paradigm maps on to those forms of critical geography that insist on the social production of place. Place, here, is not organic but part and product of a wider social and cultural framework that is, itself, exposed and revealed by the art. Such art might even be back in the gallery if its intent is to reveal the non-neutral character of the gallery as place.

Figure 5.11

about the place they are from, it is also about the travels they have been on. "Nowhereisland" was thus about displacement as much as it was about place. It was a traveling island. At the end of its journey around the coasts of Devon and Cornwall the island was destroyed and the material continued traveling as fragments were sent to the 23 003 people from 135 countries who had signed up to be citizens of this temporary nation. While "Tilted Arc" depended on being precisely where it was, "Nowhereisland" depended on a nomadic itinerary, the interrelations between places, and a lack of permanence. It performed a distributed set of sites including Svalbard, the ocean, the coast of Cornwall. It made those who encountered it think about exploration, land-grabbing, migration, and belonging in a mobile world. As James Meyer has written referring to other works: "Site as a unique, demarcated place available to perceptual experience alone – the phenomenological site of Serra or the critical site of institutional critique – becomes a network of sites referring to an elsewhere" (Meyer 2000, 30). "Nowhereisland" pointed back to a newly exposed Arctic island, to a wider geography of islands and empires, and to the acts of travel and displacement themselves.

"Nowhereisland" is certainly not the first or only artwork to insist on its own displacement. Miwon Kwon calls this kind of site-specific art nomadic. While it is clearly powered by place it is not exactly clear which place provides the power. Rather it is the relations between places. One significant piece of nomadic site-specific art was/is "When Faith Moves Mountains" by Francis Alÿs. In this work, which took place on 11 April 2002, 500 volunteers stood along a sand dune in Ventanilla, Peru, and used shovels to move a shovel-load of sand. Together they thus moved the sand dune four inches. The artwork still exists in the form of a three-screen film that was made of the event and bought by the Guggenheim Museum in New York. Clare Doherty (later to become the curator/producer of "Nowhereisland") asked some important questions of this work:

> if this work is not exactly "site-specific," why not? Though it can be removed from its original context or functional site, unlike Robert Smithson's Spiral Jetty, 1970 – one of its antecedents – it is, nevertheless, a work made in context, the product of a "situated" rather than studio-based, artistic practice. (Doherty 2004, 8)

Doherty quotes Alÿs's own account of what he intended.

> Here, we have attempted to create a kind of Land art for the landless, and, with the help of hundreds of people and shovels, we created a social allegory. This story is not validated by any physical trace or addition to the landscape. We shall now leave the care of our story to oral tradition…Only in its repetition and transmission is the work actualised. (Doherty 2004, 8)

Alÿs's work is clearly a work that engages with place. It is an intervention in a particular natural landscape that depends on an intimate interaction between the artist, people, and place. But its implications are not limited to that place – they travel between that place and time and a global, multi-sited art world – "Alÿs made a work that is embedded in the context of Ventanilla, but which is not simply about Ventanilla, Lima or Peru" (Doherty 2004, 9).

Conclusions

In this chapter we have explored some of the many ways in which conceptions of place are used in research and practice. Being informed by place involves far more than simply writing about this place or that place. It involves thinking about the implications of the idea of place for whatever it is that is being researched – the construction of memory or site-specific art for instance. By looking at research on the creation of place in a mobile world, by artists, architects, politicians, or individual domestic workers in a private room, it becomes clear that place itself has a unique and pervasive power. There is no doubt that these acts of place-creation are political and contested and researching this "politics of place" is an important strand of geographical enquiry. But the very fact that place is such a crucial site of contestation points toward its fundamental role in human life – the fact that we are placed beings. The basic unavoidability of place in human life makes it a very important object of politics. As we saw in Chapter 2, places may be socially constructed but they are necessary social constructions.

We have also seen in this chapter how the creation of places constantly connects these places to other places elsewhere. Places are not self-contained and clearly bounded units. They have horizontal connections to the world beyond. Alÿs's art work happened in a particular place but it was projected out across a global art world. The Angel Island Immigration Station museum is a unique place with a particular history but it was constructed via narratives that were national in scale. In the next chapter we move from a focus on the way places are created to focus on how they are challenged and transgressed through actions considered to be "out of place."

References

Agnew, J. A. (2002) *Place and Politics in Modern Italy*. Chicago, University of Chicago Press.

Alexander, C. (1979) *The Timeless Way of Building*. New York, Oxford University Press.

Alexander, C., Ishikawa, S., and Silverstein, M. (1977) *A Pattern Language: Towns, Buildings, Construction*. New York, Oxford University Press.

Anderson, B. (1991) *Imagined Communities: Reflections on the Origin and Spread of Nationalism*. London and New York, Verso.

Appleby, S. (1990) Crawley: A space mythology. *New Formations* 11, 19–44.

Augé, M. (1995) *Non-Places: Introduction to an Anthropology of Supermodernity*. London and New York, Verso.

Casey, E. S. (1987) *Remembering: A Phenomenological Study*. Bloomington, Indiana University Press.

Castells, M. (1996) *The Rise of the Network Society*. Cambridge, Mass., Blackwell Publishers.

Charlesworth, A. (1994) Contesting places of memory: The case of Auschwitz. *Environment and Planning D: Society and Space* 12, 579–93.

Clarke, D. (ed) (1997) *The Cinematic City*. London, Routledge.

Cook, R. (2008) Why the nation needs an Angel of the South. *The Observer*, 27 January.

Cresswell, T. and Dixon, D. (2002) *Engaging Film: Geographies of Mobility and Identity*. Lanham, Md., Rowman & Littlefield.

Day, C. (1993) *Places of the Soul: Architecture and Environmental Design as a Healing Art*. London, Aquarian/Thorsons.

Delyser, D. (2005) *Ramona Memories: Tourism and the Shaping of Southern California*. Minneapolis, University of Minnesota Press.

Deutsche, R. (1988) Uneven development: Public art in New York City. *October* 47, 3–52.

Doherty, C. (2004) *Contemporary Art: From Studio to Situation*. London, Black Dog Books.

Dovey, K. (1999) *Framing Places: Mediating Power in Built Form*. London, Routledge.

Dovey, K. (2010) *Becoming Places: Urbanism/Architecture/Identity/Power*. London, Routledge.

Duany, A., Speck, J., and Lydon, M. (2010) *The Smart Growth Manual*. New York, McGraw-Hill.

Edensor, T. (2002) *National Identity, Popular Culture and Everyday Life*. Oxford and New York, Berg.

Escobar, A. (2001) Culture sits in places: Reflections on globalism and subaltern strategies of localization. *Political Geography* 20, 139–174.

Foote, K. E. (1997) *Shadowed Ground: America's Landscapes of Violence and Tragedy*. Austin, University of Texas Press.

Frampton, K. (1985) Towards a critical regionalism: Six points for an architecture of resistance, in *Postmodern Culture*, ed. H. Foster. London, Pluto, pp. 16–30.

Gibson, W. (1984) *Neuromancer*. New York, Ace Books.

Giordano, B. (2000) Italian regionalism or "Padanian" nationalism: The political project of the Lega Nord in Italian politics. *Political Geography* 19, 445–471.

Harley, J. B. (1989) Deconstructing the map. *Cartographica* 26, 1–20.

Hawkins, H. (2013) Geography and art. An expanding field: Site, the body and practice. *Progress in Human Geography* 37, 52–71.

Hayden, D. (1995) *The Power of Place: Urban Landscapes as Public History*. Cambridge, Mass., MIT Press.

Hornstein, S. (2011) *Losing Site: Architecture, Memory and Place*. Farnham, Ashgate.

Hoskins, G. (2004) "A place to remember": Scaling the walls of Angel Island Immigration Station. *Journal of Historical Geography* 30, 685–700.

Hoskins, G. (2007) Materialising memory at Angel Island Immigration Station, San Francisco. *Environment and Planning A* 32, 437–455.

Jackson, J. B. (1994) *A Sense of Place, a Sense of Time.* New Haven, Conn., Yale University Press.

Jiven, G. and Larkham, P. J. (2003) Sense of place, authenticity and character: A commentary. *Journal of Urban Design* 8, 67–81.

Johnston, R. J. (1991) *A Question of Place: Exploring the Practice of Human Geography.* Oxford, Blackwell.

Kreider, K. (2014) *Poetics and Place: The Architecture of Sign, Subjects and Site.* London, I. B. Tauris.

Kwon, M. (1997) One place after another + Art and architecture: Notes on site specificity. *October* 80, 85–110.

Kwon, M. (2002) *One Place after Another: Site-Specific Art and Locational Identity.* Cambridge, Mass., MIT Press.

Lauretis, T. de (1990) Eccentric subjects: Feminist theory and historical consciousness. *Feminist Studies* 16, 115–150.

Leyshon, A., Matless, D., and Revill, G. (1998) *The Place of Music.* New York, Guilford Press.

Lukinbeal, C. and Zimmermann, S. (2008) *The Geography of Cinema, a Cinematic World.* Stuttgart, Steiner.

Macleod, G. and Jones, M. (2001) Renewing the geography of regions. *Environment and Planning D: Society and Space* 19, 669–695.

Massey, D. B. (1994) *Space, Place, and Gender.* Minneapolis, University of Minnesota Press.

McCullough, M. (2004) *Digital Ground: Architecture, Pervasive Computing, and Environmental Knowing.* Cambridge, Mass., MIT.

McCullough, M. (2006) On the urbanism of locative media. *Places – a Forum of Environmental Design* 18, 26–29.

McCullough, M. (2012) On attention to surroundings. *Interactions* 19, 40–49.

Meyer, J. (2000) The functional site; or, the transformation of site specificity, in *Space, Site, Intervention: Situating Installation Art*, ed. E. Suderberg. Minneapolis, University of Minnesota Press, pp. 23–38.

Meyrowitz, J. (1985) *No Sense of Place: The Impact of Electronic Media on Social Behavior.* New York, Oxford University Press.

Michalos, C. (2008) Murdering art: Destruction of art works and artist's moral rights, in *The Trials of Art*, ed. D. McClean. New York, Ram, pp. 173–193.

Mitchell, W. J. (1995) *City of Bits: Space, Place, and the Infobahn.* Cambridge, Mass., MIT Press.

Mitchell, W. J. (2003) *Me++: The Cyborg Self and the Networked City.* Cambridge, Mass., MIT Press.

Norberg-Schulz, C. (1980) *Genius Loci: Towards a Phenomenology of Architecture.* London, Academy Editions.

Norberg-Schulz, C. (1985) *The Concept of Dwelling: On the Way to Figurative Architecture.* New York, Rizzoli.

Norberg-Schulz, C. (2000) *Architecture: Presence, Language, and Place*. Milan, Skira.

Paasi, A. (1996) *Territories, Boundaries, and Consciousness: The Changing Geographies of the Finnish–Russian Border*. Chichester, John Wiley & Sons.

Paasi, A. (2002) Place and region: Regional worlds and words. *Progress in Human Geography* 26, 802–811.

Pratt, G. (1999) Geographies of identity and difference: Marking boundaries, in *Human Geography Today*, ed. D. Massey, J. Allen, and P. Sarre. Cambridge, Polity, pp. 151–168.

Prieto, E. (2013) *Literature, Geography, and the Postmodern Poetics of Place*. New York, Palgrave Macmillan.

Reid, L. and Smith, N. (1993) John Wayne meets Donald Trump: The Lower East Side as Wild Wild West, in *Selling Places: The City as Cultural Capital, Past and Present*, ed. G. Kearns and C. Philo. Oxford, Pergamon, pp. 193–209.

Rose, G. (1993) *Feminism and Geography: The Limits of Geographical Knowledge*. Cambridge, Polity.

Royal Academy of Arts (2013) *Richard Rogers RA: Inside Out*. Exhibition catalogue. Online. Available at static.royalacademy.org.uk/files/richard-rogers-room-9-hr-1675.pdf (accessed 8 May 2014).

Sternberg, E. M. (2009) *Healing Spaces: The Science of Place and Well-Being*. Cambridge, Mass., Belknap Press of Harvard University Press.

Suderburg, E. (2000) *Space, Site, Intervention: Situating Installation Art*. Minneapolis, University of Minnesota Press.

Taylor, P. J. (1999) *Modernities: A Geohistorical Interpretation*. Cambridge, Polity Press.

Till, K. (1993) Neotraditional towns and urban villages: The cultural production of a geography of "otherness." *Environment and Planning D: Society and Space* 11, 709–732.

Till, K. E. (2005) *The New Berlin: Memory, Politics, Place*. Minneapolis, University of Minnesota Press.

Tschumi, B. (1994) *Architecture and Disjunction*. Cambridge, Mass., MIT Press.

Tuan, Y.-F. (1991) A view of geography. *Geographical Review* 81, 99–107.

Wakeford, N. (1999) Gender and the landscapes of computing in an Internet cafe, in *Virtual Geographies: Bodies, Space and Relations*, ed. M. Crang, P. Crang, and J. May. London, Routledge, pp. 178–202.

Wilken, R. and Goggin, G. (2012) *Mobile Technology and Place*. New York, Routledge.

Zook, M. A. and Graham, M. (2007a) The creative reconstruction of the Internet: Google and the privatization of cyberspace and DigiPlace. *Geoforum* 38, 1322–1343.

Zook, M. A. and Graham, M. (2007b) Mapping DigiPlace: Geocoded Internet data and the representation of place. *Environment and Planning B-Planning and Design* 34, 466–482.

6

Working with Place – Anachorism

The creation of place necessarily involves the definition of what lies outside. To put it another way the "outside" plays a crucial role in the definition of the "inside." In many of the examples of place at work in Chapter 5 there was a clear sense of a politics of place production. Rancho Santa Margarita, for instance, has been based on stories that exclude women, black people, and Native-Americans (among others). The creation of "Padania" in Italy by the Northern League has been based on the designation of the Italian South as the "other." In this chapter we will consider the use of place in research concerning the politics of place and its role in defining what is appropriate and what is not.

We have repeatedly seen how place is a word that is used often in everyday speech. As such, its meaning appears as common sense and its assumptions are taken for granted. Many of these everyday uses link hierarchies in society with spatial location and arrangement. Someone can be "put in her place" or is supposed to "know his place." There is, we are told, "a place for everything and everything in its place." Such uses of the term place suggest a tight connection between geographical place and assumptions about normative behavior. Things, people, and practices, it seems, can be "in-place" or "out-of-place" (Cresswell 1996).

When something or someone has been judged to be "out-of-place," they have committed a transgression. Transgression simply means "crossing a line." Unlike the sociological definition of "deviance," transgression is an inherently spatial idea. The line that is crossed is often a geographical line and a socio-cultural one. It may or may not be the case that the

Place: An Introduction, Second Edition. Tim Cresswell.
© 2015 John Wiley & Sons, Ltd. Published 2015 by John Wiley & Sons, Ltd.

transgression was intended by the perpetrator. What matters is that the action is seen as transgression by someone who is disturbed by it.

Often, when people, things, and practices are seen as "out-of-place" they are described as pollution and dirt. The anthropologist Mary Douglas defined dirt as "matter out-of-place." To be "out-of-place" depends on the pre-existence of a classification system of some kind.

> Shoes are not dirty in themselves, but it is dirty to place them on the dining table; food is not dirty in itself, but it is dirty to leave cooking utensils in the bedroom, or food bespattered on clothing, similarly, bathroom equipment in the drawing room; clothes lying on chairs. (Douglas 1966, 36)

The stronger the spatial classification – the greater the desire to expel and exclude – the easier it is to upset those who invest in an existing order. The construction of places, in other words, forms the basis for the possibility of transgression or, in Douglas's terms, pollution. Just as we have a term for thinking about things in the wrong time – ana*chron*ism – we might invent a term for things in the wrong place – ana*chor*ism.

The use of place to produce order leads to the unintended consequence of place becoming an object and tool of resistance to that order – new types of deviance and transgression such as strikes and sit-ins become possible. The clearer the established meaning and practices of a particular place the easier it is to transgress the expectations that come with place. This is one reason why anti-globalization protestors frequently pick McDonald's as a target. It is a very clear and well-understood symbol of global capital and the kinds of consumption practices that it encourages. It is why any number of recent mass protests and revolutionary movements use well-known public squares such as Tahrir Square in Cairo, or Independence Square in Kiev, to make their point. It isn't just that it is a space capable of holding a large number of people, it is because these squares are places with layers of pre-existing meaning that gives the protests added potency.

Since the mid-1980s there has been an explosion of work which considers the role of place in the production of outsiders – the exclusion of people (and more recently, animals (Philo 1995)) who are said to be "out-of-place." Mad people (Philo 1987, Parr and Philo 1995), gypsy-travelers (Sibley 1981, Halfacree 1996), children (Philo 1992, Valentine 1997), political protestors (Cresswell 1994), non-white people (Craddock 2000, Anderson 1991), gay, lesbian, and bisexual people (Bell and Valentine 1995, Brown 2000), the homeless (Cresswell 2001, Veness 1992), prostitutes (Hubbard 2000), the disabled (Kitchin 1998) and a plethora of "others" have all been described by the media, local authorities, national governments, and others as "out-of-place" – as not matching the expected relations between place, meanings and practice. Rather than review this whole body of literature I will, instead, focus on animals, the homeless, and, first, sexuality "out-of-place."

Sexuality Out-of-Place

The term sexuality refers to the social identities that are built around different forms of sexual desire. Sexualities, in other words, are not just signifiers of different kinds of sexual practice but forms of complicated social and cultural relations. At first glance many people do not see a link between sexuality and place. But like any other form of social relation (class, gender, race, etc.) it is constituted, in part, geographically. It is fairly commonplace for instance, to hear people suggest that gay sexuality is fine just so long as it does not occur in public places. This was more or less the party line of the government of Russia in its recent attempt to outlaw the "promotion" of homosexuality. Promotion apparently included public displays of gay affection. To back up this argument it might be claimed that heterosexuality belongs "at home" or "in the bedroom" so homosexuality does too.

Much of the work on sexuality in geography has sought to show how such claims are absurd. Heterosexuality occurs everywhere (Duncan 1996). Straight people feel free to kiss in public or walk down the street hand in hand. Public spaces such as law courts and government offices formally institutionalize hetero-relations while making gay relationships illegal in some countries. Everywhere we look straight sexuality is accepted as normal and is thus invisible to straight people. Gay people, on the other hand, see heterosexuality everywhere and through this experience their own sexuality as radically "out-of-place." All it takes is for a gay couple to kiss in a public place for hetero-outrage to come to the fore. The geographer Michael Brown has studied the spatiality of gay sexuality at length. His book *Closet Space* examines the ways in which gay sexuality is maginalized and made invisible at all scales (Brown 2000). He describes a scene on a bus in which these tensions and expectations are made dramatically clear.

> The Seattle Metro bus no. 7 stopped abruptly to pick up two very wet people just at the crest of Capitol Hill on a rainy Tuesday afternoon. The sudden

braking caught everyone's attention, and broke the passionate soul kissing of a man and woman sitting just across from me. Since I was sitting towards the rear of the dingy bus, I had a long view of a slender, trendy woman making her way purposefully down the aisle. Behind her, I heard her companion before I could see him. We all could, because he was speaking so loudly. With a mixture of aplomb and hubris our new rider proclaimed, "That's right, people, I'm swinging my hips as I walk on by. And if you don't like it, you can kiss my beautiful queer ass!" With regal camp he sashayed down the aisle, past my seat, never once breaking his stare forward. On the other side of the aisle, the young heterosexual couple "tsked," huffed and "Oh, Gawwwwd"-ed this young gay man audibly enough to make their revulsion clear to those of us in the back of the bus. "Who said that?" the gay man demanded loudly.

Everyone on the bus began to grow visibly uncomfortable. After all, this was Seattle. "I did," the woman stated loud and clear, but without turning to face him. Then she whispered something inaudible to her boyfriend and they both laughed. "Well if you don't like it, girlfriend, *what the hell you doin'* up on Capitol Hill in the first place!" (Brown 2000, 27)

As Brown observes, there is a complicated set of interactions between the performance of sexuality and expectations about place in this event. To the heterosexual couple all space is straight space. Places such as the city and the bus sustained heteronormativity – the idea that heterosexuality is normal, natural, and appropriate. They felt that they could kiss passionately in public. The gay man, to them, was acting out-of-place – disturbing the unspoken rules of sexuality. To the gay man, however, this was Capitol Hill, a gay area in Seattle. To him the straight couple were "out-of-place" and should consider keeping their sexuality, and certainly their homophobia, "in the closet." The idea of the closet is a complicated one which acts at all scales "from the body to the globe" (the subtitle of Brown's book). This metaphorical closet is both a place of secrecy and a place of autonomy and safety. The closet is a place where a person can keep their sexuality entirely to themselves or it can, more literally, become a building or an area of the city where it is safe to be gay. It can also be a confining prison.

This issue of the closet and heteronormative space has become central to the geographical analysis of sexuality. Geographers have asked why some places seem to be safe places for certain sexualities to be performed while other places pressure gays, lesbians, and bisexuals to keep their sexualities to themselves. The work of Gill Valentine has been central to this line of thinking. She has shown how lesbians have had to consistently conceal their sexuality in certain kinds of places – particularly home and work – in order to avoid discrimination and hatred. The women she has interviewed reveal incredibly complicated daily lives of concealment in some places and being "out" in others. Some of them had to travel miles to feel comfortable away from both family (parents and siblings) and workmates (Valentine 1993).

There are many different identities gay, lesbian, and bisexual people can choose to perform, just as there are many identities straight people can perform (hell's angel, "new man," power-dresser, etc.). David Bell, John Binnie, Julia Cream, and Gill Valentine explore two of these identities, the "gay skinhead" and the "lipstick lesbian," in their paper "All hyped up and no place to go":

> Through the deployment of the "gay skinhead" and "lipstick lesbian" and the places they produce and occupy, we hope to illuminate the "unnaturalness" of both heterosexual everyday space and masculine and feminine hetero-sexual identities associated with them. The exposure of the fabrication of both seamless heterosexual identities and the straight spaces they occupy should shatter the illusion of their just *being*, of simply naturally occurring. (Bell *et al.* 1994, 32, emphasis in original)

A "lipstick lesbian" is a lesbian who dresses in a hyper-feminine way, thus challenging the popular conception of lesbian women as masculine figures. The figure of the lipstick lesbian, to some people, mocks heterosexual expressions of femininity in a way that is more subtle than the butch drag of other lesbians. Their appearance, it is claimed, "undermines a hetero-sexual's ability to determine whether feminine women in everyday spaces are lesbian or heterosexual" (Bell *et al.* 1994, 42). This uncertainty, created by images of femininity in heterosexual places, means that straight people can no longer assume the accepted codes of everyday life and thus hetero-sexual places are undermined. In a twist to the tale, though, the authors acknowledge that this subversion depends on straight people being aware of the existence of lipstick lesbians in the first place. Since most straight people assume the normal and natural condition of heteronormativity, it seems likely that most of them are unaware of the subversions going on around them. To wake them out of their slumber they are more likely to be provoked by the gay man on Brown's bus in Seattle.

A transgressive act that was definitely noticed was the Greenham Common Women's Peace Camp (near Newbury, in Berkshire, southern England) in the early 1980s. Women camped outside the US Air Force base from 1981 onwards to protest the cruise missiles that were being based there. In their view the cruise missiles, armed with nuclear warheads, were "out-of-place" in the United Kingdom. Soon local residents of nearby Newbury, Berkshire, began to object to the peace camp. Government figures and the media, for a period of several years, used every metaphor they could think of to describe the women as "out-of-place." These included obligatory references to dirt, disease, madness, and, of course, sexuality (Cresswell 1994).

The Sun (19 November 1983) claimed that the women "are not people – they're all burly lesbians." News reports frequently suggested that the fact that this was an all women's camp automatically meant that the vast majority of the protesters were lesbians. The fact that they dressed in "masculine" clothes and were frequently dirty only seemed to confirm this impression. The *Daily Mail* (13 January 1983) paints a picture of multiple transgression:

> And there's Eve breastfeeding by the fire, a vague, amiable, ever smiling lesbian mother from Islington who's camping here with her two children, aged eight and six months by different fathers, one of them West Indian. (Quoted in Cresswell 1994, 49)

Eve is clearly a figure "out-of-place" here. She is breastfeeding in a public place, she is a lesbian, and she has children with multiple fathers including one (we must assume) who is black.

> [H]alf the women I lived among at Greenham were lesbians, striding the camp with their butch haircuts, boots and boilersuits. They flaunt their sexuality, boast about it, joke about it. And some take delight in proclaiming their loathing of men...I was shocked on my first day when two peace women suddenly went into passionate embrace in full view of everyone...And gradually I became annoyed at the way doting couples sat around the camp fire kissing and caressing...A lot of women "go gay" after arriving at the camp. With no men around they have to turn to each other for comfort. (Quoted in Cresswell 1994, 50)

Here, the *Daily Express's* undercover investigator, Sarah Bond, acts in the same way as the woman on the bus described by Brown. She sees women kissing in a place she considers inappropriate and is disgusted – she described it as flaunting. Do straight people "flaunt" their sexuality when they kiss in a public place? Bond is arguing that this kind of activity should be put back into the closet – should be re*placed*. To Bond, lesbian sexuality is "out-of-place" at Greenham Common. The reference to the absence of men at the end of the extract implies that women only turn to each other in places without men. Behind this lies the missing place of "home" where husbands would undoubtedly be available for "comfort."

The understanding of sexualities-out-of-place should not be restricted to supposedly marginal sexualities. Ignoring heterosexualities only serves to reinforce the notion that heterosexuality is normal and thus invisible (Hubbard 2000). For the most part heterosexual activity and the wider sense of identity that surrounds it remain the norm by which other forms of sexuality are implicitly and explicitly judged. The idea of "home," for instance, the ideal place, is quite clearly heteronormative. Recent research has shown how the idea of home and actual homes themselves are constructed as places for traditional families. Homeliness does not properly arrive until the children arrive (Valentine 1993). It is this heterosexual home that lies behind many of the descriptions of the Greenham women as "out-of-place."

Some of the most interesting work on sexuality and place has been on heterosexual prostitution. Research has shown how prostitution is seen as "out-of-place" in some places while it is almost acceptable in others (Hubbard 1998). Philip Hubbard has outlined a number of arguments about the "place" of prostitution in England. He notes that there is a generally recognized distinction between "high-class" prostitutes who work in "private" spaces and "lower-class" prostitutes who work on the street and in public space. While the former are usually ignored, due to the assumption that sexuality gets expressed in private spaces (an illusion shown to be false by queer theorists in particular), the latter have been the object of considerable moral panics in British cities such as Birmingham and Bradford where local residents' groups have enacted pickets of prostitutes in order to curb what they see as a public nuisance.

The law in Britain seeks to make prostitution in public places less visible but, as Hubbard argues, "dominant moral geographies appear to dictate this visibility is more acceptable in some spaces than others" (Hubbard 1997, 133). These spaces where prostitution is deemed to be "in-place" are commonly known as red-light districts. These places are typically in economically marginal spaces of the city and can, in Hubbard's terms be seen as "a part of a continuing (but contested) process involving the exclusion of disorderly prostitution from orderly sexuality (or 'bad girls' from 'good girls'), removing prostitutes from areas where they would stand out as unnatural or deviant, potentially 'polluting' civilised society" (Hubbard 1997, 135). Hubbard reveals how policing strategies often overlook prostitution in designated areas or "toleration zones" in order that they might better exclude prostitutes from elsewhere. Thus places of abjection are created and tolerated on the margins of city centers.

In work on the geography of sexuality the word "place" is often used interchangeably with the word "space." It is important to bear in mind, therefore, the specific analytical qualities of place that make it important in these studies. The idea of being "out-of-place" or "in-place" is admittedly a simple one, but one that nonetheless conveys a sense of the way segments of the geographical world are meaningful and how those meanings both produce and are reproduced by people and their practices. A saying from Sri Lanka states; "The fish don't talk about the water." What this means is that we rarely explicitly become aware of and talk about that which we take for granted. To a fish the water is their taken-for-granted world. People have environments too – environments made up of meaningful places. What the geographers of sexuality have shown us is that these places, more often than not, contribute to the invisible and unstated normalization and naturalization of particular kinds of sexuality. Other kinds of sexuality – gay, lesbian, bisexual, commercial – threaten the links between space, meaning, and practice that make up "place" and suggest other ways of being, other possible meanings, new kinds of place.

The first edition of this book was published in 2004. In the ten years between then and now there have been some remarkable developments in Europe and North America regarding the visibility of queer sexuality. In many instances places have become less heteronormative as governments at local and national levels have legislated to allow gay marriage and/or to make violence against gay, lesbian, bisexual, or transgender individuals a hate crime. The first legal same-sex marriages in modern times occurred in Ontario, Canada, in 2001 but were only made retroactively legal in 2003 – just as I was finishing the first edition of this book. As I write, 18 nations have legalized same-sex marriage and it is now legal in 18 of the United States of America. Clearly this does not mean that all places in these countries and states are now magically LGBTQ (Lesbian, Gay, Bisexual, Trans, Queer) friendly but, nevertheless, the geographies of sexuality are clearly changing. It is also important to bear in mind that in many parts of the world it is becoming more difficult to be openly gay. This has become famously true in Russia. As I write (February 2014), Uganda has just passed draconian anti-gay laws. Today a newspaper in Uganda has published a list of 200 "top homos."

The Homeless – People without Place

Place plays a particularly powerful role in the labeling and treatment of people who appear to be mobile, without place, of no fixed abode. The idea of "home" as an ideal kind of place has particularly negative consequences for the homeless. In his 1991 paper "A view of geography" Yi-Fu Tuan described geography as the study of Earth as the home of people (Tuan 1991). The central concept for Tuan is "home."

> Home obviously means more than a natural or physical setting. Especially, the term cannot be limited to a built place. A useful point of departure for understanding home may be not its material manifestation but rather a concept: home is a unit of space organized mentally and materially to satisfy a people's real and perceived basic biosocial needs and, beyond that, their higher aesthetic-political aspirations. (Tuan 1991, 102)

In other words home, for Tuan, is a kind of ideal place. "Home, insofar as it is an intimately lived in place, is imbued with moral meaning" (Tuan 1991, 105). These reflections on place as home are, of course, open to critique at the theoretical level. We have already seen how feminists, for instance, have argued that home is often far from the cozy moral universe Tuan suggests. Indeed home can be an oppressive, confining, and even terrifying place for many people – especially for abused women and children. Earlier in this chapter we say how the idealized view of home is one based around a heterosexual family. But the perception of place as home also has consequences for those without readily apparent places to call home.

Anthropologist Liisa Malkki has argued that there is a tendency in the modern world to locate people and identities in particular spaces and within particular boundaries (Malkki 1992). He belongs there, she belongs here. One result of this is to think of people without place in wholly negative ways. Connected to this, she goes on, are ways of thinking which are also rooted and bounded. She suggests that it is our incessant desire to divide the world up into clearly bounded territorial units which produces a "sedentarist metaphysics." Fixed, bounded, and rooted conceptions of culture and identity, she argues, are linked to particular ways of thinking which are themselves sedentary. These ways of thinking then reaffirm and enable the common-sense segmentation of the world into things like nations, states, counties, and places. Thinking of the world as rooted and bounded is reflected in language and social practice. Such thoughts actively territorialize identities in property, in region, in nation – in place – and they simultaneously produce thoughts and practices that treat mobility and displacement as pathological. Malkki provides the example of a post-war report of refugees:

> Homelessness is a serious threat to moral behaviour…At the moment the refugee crosses the frontiers of his own world, his whole moral outlook, his attitude toward the divine order of things, changes… [The refugees'] conduct makes it obvious that we are dealing with individuals who are basically amoral, without any sense of personal or social responsibility…They no longer feel themselves bound by ethical precepts which every honest citizen… respects. They become a menace, dangerous characters who will stop at nothing. (Quoted in Malkki 1992, 32)

Here we see a clear connection made between people moving out of the place they "belong" and perceived amorality and danger. In this sense, place is much more than a thing in the world – it also frames our ways of seeing and understanding the world. In philosophical terms, place is more than a question of ontology (what exists) but, perhaps more fundamentally, a question of epistemology (how we know things). One way in which place as a concept can be used empirically and theoretically, then, is to look at "people without place." Consider the homeless and refugees.

Home and homelessness

Homelessness has, as far as we know, always been present in human society in one form or another. To be homeless does not simply mean to be without what we (inhabitants of the contemporary developed world for the most part) would call a home. Homelessness is very much defined by a certain kind of disconnection from particular forms of place. Historians and theorists often point to the English vagrancy scares of Elizabethan times as an important historical point in the formation of ideas about homelessness. It was at this time that a large number of people, formerly tied to the land of their masters, were freed from feudal ties and started to wander the land. They were known as "masterless men" which meant both that they served no lord and that they were "without place." Here place means both a geographical location and a clear place in a social hierarchy that was beginning to dissolve. The sociologist Zygmunt Bauman described these vagabonds as "the advanced troops or guerilla units of post-traditional chaos…and they had to go if order…was to be the rule. The free-roaming vagabonds made the search for new, state-managed, societal-level order imperative and urgent" (Bauman 1995, 94).

One element of this transformation – from feudalism to early capitalism – was the displacement of thousands of people from the land and the villages they had formerly belonged to. These "vagrants" and "masterless men" created a new measure of uncertainty about the traditional patterns of rights and duties. In short they were seen as people without place and were thus a threat to the most fundamental forms of order.

> What made the vagabond so terrifying was his apparent freedom to move and so to escape the net of the previously locally based control. Worse than that, the movements of the vagabond were unpredictable; unlike the pilgrim or, for that matter, a nomad, the vagabond has no set destination. You do not know where he will move next, because he himself does not know or care much. (Bauman 1995, 94)

The mobility of the vagabond is key for Bauman. Unlike other mobile people, such as tourists and nomads, the vagabond's mobility was totally unpredictable and thus threatening. The vagabond's wayward travels meant that he always had traces of elsewhere about him which disturbed those who had chosen a settled and rooted existence – the vagabond threatened to undo the comforts of place and transgressed the expectations of a sedentarist metaphysics.

While we rarely talk of vagrancy in the twenty-first century, homelessness is still very much a contentious issue throughout the world. What has not changed is the fact that homelessness cannot be understood adequately without recourse to an examination of the kinds of places that produce it. While Elizabethan vagrancy needs to be seen in the light of feudal understandings of the place of the poor, contemporary homelessness needs to be seen in relation to the kinds of places that are being produced in the contemporary city and countryside.

Neil Smith has researched and written about the homeless in Tompkins Square Park in New York's Lower East Side during the 1980s and 1990s (Smith 1996). It was at this time that Mayor Dinkins tried to remove the homeless from the park. We saw in Chapter 5 how the control of public space was one aspect of the wider processes of gentrification. The Lower East Side had been an area of the city ignored by the city government and by business. Low property prices had attracted middle-class gentrifiers back into the area. The new "yuppie" residents had a particular vision of the kind of place they wanted to live in and it did not include homeless people in "their" park. The homeless were perceived and represented as a threat to both their personal safety and, perhaps more importantly, their property values. It was in this context that Dinkins attempted to remove the homeless people who spent the night in the park. He used the dictionary definition of "park" to make his point:

> A park is not a shantytown. It is not a campground, a homeless shelter, a shooting gallery for drug addicts or political problem. Unless it is Tompkins Square Park in Manhattan's East Village. (Mayor Dinkins quoted in Smith 1996, 220)

Here Dinkins is making a direct claim about the kind of place a park is. This kind of place, he is arguing, is not the kind of place you sleep in. For this reason the park needed to be reclaimed from the homeless.

This line of argument is remarkably similar to that of his predecessor, Mayor Koch, who had also been annoyed by the sight of the homeless in his city (Koch had actually begun the process of removing the homeless from Tompkins Square, calling the park a "cesspool"). Reacting to the presence of the homeless in Grand Central Station, he had attempted to introduce an anti-loitering law giving the police the powers to remove the homeless from public spaces. The State Supreme Court had overturned the law and Koch had responded in a speech to the American Institute of Architects. In the question and answer session at the end of the speech Koch reminded the architects of the homeless people in Grand Central Station.

> These homeless people, you can tell who they are. They're sitting on the floor, occasionally defecating, urinating, talking to themselves…We thought it would be reasonable for the authorities to say, "you can't stay here unless you're here for transportation." Reasonable, rational people would come to the same conclusion, right? Not the Court of Appeals. (Mayor Koch quoted in Deutsche 1988, 5)

Both Koch and Dinkins are making arguments about the meaning of place in their tirades against the homeless. Koch claims that "reasonable people" would agree that a railroad station is a place for traveling. Dinkins uses the authority of *Webster's Dictionary* to point out that the definition of park does not include a place to sleep. Both of them, by making these appeals to "common sense," take the issue of homelessness out of its wider context in the economic and political geography of New York City. The right-wing critic George Will went even further when he wrote in 1988 that:

> It is illegal to litter the streets, frankly it ought to be illegal…to sleep in the streets. Therefore, there is a simple matter of public order and hygiene in getting these people somewhere else. Not arrest them, but move them off somewhere where they are simply out of sight. (George Will quoted in Smith 1996, 28)

Homelessness is treated simply as instances of "people out-of-place" – as a human form of litter – rather than as a symptom of the urban politics and economics of New York. As Neil Smith, Rosalyn Deutsche, and others have argued, to answer questions about homelessness we need to look at the city as a social space in which homelessness occurs; spaces of the city reveal the conditions that produce homelessness. Homelessness is produced through the push to reconstruct the city as a cohesive place according to middle-class/elite values.

But it is not only the city where the homeless are seen as "out-of-place." Paul Cloke, Paul Milbourne, and Rebekah Widdowfield have collaborated on a project to examine the connection that is usually made between urban places and homelessness – a connection that, in their view, makes rural homelessness all but invisible (Cloke *et al.* 2000). Very few academic considerations of homelessness have focused on rural homelessness. Homelessness, it seems, has its place – and that place is the city. The countryside – the rural – has most often been seen as a place away from the problems of urbanity. It is for this reason that the street names of Crawley (see Chapter 5) were so bucolic. The countryside is portrayed as a problem-free realm of peace and tranquility. This image of the rural, known as the "rural idyll," has deep roots in British history with the romantic vision of a "green and pleasant land." This image has, of course, changed over recent years with issues such as mad cow and foot and mouth disease and the increasing visibility of rural poverty. Nevertheless, rural homelessness has hardly been a headline issue. As Cloke *et al.* remark, there are morphological and socio-cultural reasons for the "noncoupling of homelessness and rurality" (Cloke *et al.* 2000, 718). Morphologically, rural places simply do not provide the kinds of spaces where homeless people might gather and become visible. In addition some of the rural homeless choose to spend their nights under hedges and in the woods where they will not be seen and harassed. Socio-culturally, rural residents often deny that problems exist in the areas they inhabit. Here the pervasive myth of the rural idyll seems to be strong still. An interview with Louie, a parish councillor from Devon, in England, illustrates this problem:

INTERVIEWER: Do you know of any problems of homelessness in the
              village?

LOUIE: There isn't any homelessness here. We have a good,
              helpful community. If folks are in trouble we help
              them. All the undesirables keep themselves to
              themselves or move away. We've had some lovely
              people come to live here.

INTERVIEWER: What would you do if you saw a homeless person in the
              village?

LOUIE: Well I'd die of shock, I think. We just don't get that round
              here – in Exeter maybe, but not out here.

As the authors point out, Louie can only contemplate homelessness by displacing it to the urban environment of Exeter. The countryside has been constituted by both its inhabitants and by policymakers and government officials as a "pure space." Cloke *et al.* draw on the work of David Sibley to make this point:

the countryside, it seems, belongs to the middle class, to landowners and to people who engage in blood sports. A rigid stereotype of place, the English countryside, throws up discrepant others. These groups are other, they are folk-devils, and they transgress only because the countryside is defined as a stereotypical pure space which cannot accommodate difference. (Sibley quoted in Cloke *et al.* 2000, 727)

Another aspect of rural place that Cloke *et al.* draw our attention to is the tight connection between the very idea of "home" and rurality. Part of the rural idyll is a particular idea of domesticity and family. This is as true of the Cotswolds as it is of rural Iowa, with the well-known imagery of "mom and apple pie." "Being without a home, then, in geographic space where the *imagined* geography is one where the home is valorized to this extent, is once again to transgress the sociocultural meanings and moralities which lie at the heart of rural life" (Cloke *et al.* 2000, 730).

This connection between home and rurality was also evident in reactions to the tramp in the United States in the latter part of the nineteenth century and the first three decades of the twentieth century. Following the economic collapse of 1873 and the completion of the first transcontinental railroad in 1869 many people were made homeless. For the first time they were mobile on a continental scale – able to move from coast to coast within a week or two. These people were called tramps. One reaction to them was to label them a threat to women in rural homes. Stories circulated about tramps coming to doors at night, when the man of the house was away, and threatening women and the domesticity they embodied. The *Philadelphia Press* of 14 July 1907 reported that "the newspapers have each day printed one instance, often two, of women walking... in the rural districts of Eastern Pennsylvania or Southern New Jersey, who have fled in terror from some tramp or vagrant" (quoted in Cresswell 2001, 93). The biggest threat, though, was thought to be the moment when the tramp visited the home. Henry Rood in *The Forum* in 1889 observed that there are "few mothers and fewer daughters who, under such circumstances, would refuse to give food or clothing to a burly, unkempt tramp, who accompanied his request with threatening expression" (quoted in Cresswell 2001, 94). This moment of threat was also the subject of cartoons and posters. An illustration in *Harper's* magazine in 1876 shows a pathetic but threatening tramp asking for money or food while a motherly figure retreats with wooden spoon in hand. The table is laid and dinner is cooking. Outside other men wander. The home, a place at the heart of American national mythology, was clearly under threat from the homeless.

In a more profound way homelessness is very much a product of the idea of "home" as a particular kind of place. In the Western world "home" is an ideal as well as a place – a spatially constructed ideology usually correlated with housing. At its most basic level, homelessness denotes a lack of housing. But homelessness also signifies "displacement" – an existential lack that is perhaps even more fundamental than being without shelter. Jon May explores this notion of "home as place" through an exploration of the life histories of people living in various forms of shelter for the homeless (May 2000). His interviews with these men often evoke a sense of loss-of-place far deeper than simply the loss of a home in a restricted sense. Take his interview with Michael for instance:

Figure 6.1   Illustration from *Harper's* magazine (1876). Here the domestic space of the home, complete with woman, child, and dinner on the table, is threatened by the tramp who comes to the door.

INTERVIEWER: Why leave London?'

MICHAEL: I dunno. I just wanted some place new. Get out of it. I was fed up with it [long pause]. You know, erm, I probably didn't think about it to be honest…I wasn't going to stay where I was [in a hostel following the separation from his wife] so I said, well, "anywhere has got to be better than this."

INTERVIEWER: So moving wasn't like a wrench for you?

MICHAEL: No, I wouldn't say that [it wasn't as if] I was leaving anything behind, you know? I mean you've just got to pack your bags and you're off.

INTERVIEWER: And does this feel like your town now?

MICHAEL: [Ironic laughter] I don't know [pause]. Yeah, I suppose it is – at the moment…But at the end of the day you always talk about "going home" don't you?…I mean, I've made friends with a few people [pause] you know,

go for a drink and that. Fine, but…no, I wouldn't call
this place my home…where you come from's home
isn't it?
(Interview with Michael, age 33, 4 December 1997, in May 2000, 748)

As May argues, the notion of displacement suggests a previous experience of home as place, "one reaching beyond the boundaries of residence to include that wider sense of belonging more usually described as a 'sense of place'" (May 2000, 748).

But as April Veness has shown, homelessness is also a term of disrespect for those who do not fit into a conception of home – who do not fit prevailing standards of housing, land tenure, family form, and material comfort (Veness 1992). Through both historical research and ethnographic work with homeless people, Veness shows how what counts as "home" has historically shrunk and boundaries have become more rigid. Forms of housing such as council (government) housing, trailers/mobile homes, shelters, bedsits, and student lodging have become increasingly suspect, particularly since World War II. All of these appear to be less-than-home within an ideology that equates the notion of home with private homeownership. Even then it is preferable that the home is a detached one. This ideology of home can be seen in British Prime Minister Margaret Thatcher's "right to buy" scheme in the 1980s, when council-house owners were told that they would not really have a proper home unless they owned it. Home is very much a category that defines normality.

As "home" became increasingly restrictive in the kind of shelter that it applied to so more and more people became "homeless." Simultaneously the homeless appeared to be more and more transgressive as their lives were out of compliance with the rosy ideology of the property pages. Some of the homeless people Veness and May talk to think of themselves as having places to call home – even when they were sleeping rough – but these places simply do not count in the eyes of those who encounter them. The close connection between place, identity and morality creates a world that is difficult for some of those who are apparently "without place."

Refugees

Refugees and asylum-seekers are at the center of the moral panic of the age. Seemingly daily we hear about asylum-seekers entering the UK through the Channel Tunnel, Afghans trying to get into Australia, North Africans into Italy, or Mexicans into the United States. Rarely, on the other hand, do we (here in the Western world) hear about the refugees in Pakistan (for instance), where the numbers involved are much larger. Reporting on refugees in recent times points towards the comparative over-abundance of reporting on refugees as a "crisis." In many cases the argument is made for measures to crack down on the refugees and asylum-seekers so that it is not so "easy" for them to enter Britain, Italy, or Australia. At first glance we might suppose that the idea of "place" is not particularly relevant to understanding this issue. But, as with the homeless, ideas about place are right at the heart of the definition of refugees as a "problem" – as people "out-of-place."

Despite the seemingly contemporary nature of the refugee "problem" it is necessary to see the refugee as an historical figure. The following is a précis of the history given by Saskia Sassen in her book *Guests and Aliens* (Sassen 1999). Refugee is a term specifically designed to refer to Protestants who were forced to leave France at the end of the seventeenth century. By the eighteenth century the term was being more widely used to describe anyone leaving his or her country in times of distress. By the nineteenth century it was usually used to refer to well-educated elites who had left their homeland such as Polish aristocrats in France. It was towards the end of the nineteenth century that large numbers of relatively poor refugees became a feature of European life. The Franco-Prussian wars alone (1864–1871) created huge numbers of displaced people with twelve million men fighting against France.

As nation-states became a feature of European life, anxieties grew about being ruled by "foreigners." When the Germans took over Alsace-Lorraine, France expelled 80,000 Germans and 130,000 French people left for France. Often these were poor refugees – working class and often politically radical. Even so, many places welcomed them as extra labor. At the same time the industrial revolution and the end of serfdom in Austria (1848) and Russia (1861) were transforming European geographies of movement. Masses of people were newly mobile. The construction of railroads in Europe, for instance, made use of migrant workers from Ireland, Italy and elsewhere. Outside of Europe, colonialism meant mass migration overseas. Between 1840 and 1900, 26 million people left Europe. For many, the new mass geographical mobility did not correspond to social mobility.

In this the condition of the new migrants approached, again, that of the political refugees. The struggle for survival consumed their energies rather than a coherent narrative of ambition. For the new masses of migrants and refugees, the geography of movement became a vector of change without a secure destination. They revolved on fortune's wheel, rather than pursued a fate. (Sassen 1999, 45)

By World War I over two million Jews had left Eastern Europe and many more refugees had been created by the Ottoman Empire. The concept of "foreigner" or "outsider" began to connote allegiance to states.

World War II signaled the emergence of the modern refugee crisis. State sovereignty became a central form of power and borders were increasingly policed. Passports were more or less invented around this time. An inward looking United States made it harder and harder for refugees and migrants to enter the country and this forced Europeans to deal with refugees coming from the East. Refugees were increasingly seen as people who did not belong to the host national society and therefore were not entitled to rights of citizenship. Citizenship was tied to place. As with vagabonds and transients before them, this "being without place" was a source of anxiety. The state reacted to this anxiety by identifying them and regulating them.

What this pocket history shows us is that the refugee is a profoundly European product – founded on the organization of the nation-state at the turn of the century in Europe. The drawing and policing of national borders, the firming up of state sovereignty and the construction of national identities were all necessary conditions for the production of the refugee as a person "out-of-place." The place they were out of was the nation and that was itself a relatively recent phenomenon.

The modern refugee is legally defined by Article 1 of the Geneva Convention Relating to the Status of Refugees, 1951 and the 1967 New York Protocol to the Convention Relating to the Status of Refugees. The relevant passage reads as follows:

> Owing to a well-founded fear of being persecuted for reasons of race, religion, nationality, membership of a social group or political opinion, is *outside the country of his nationality* and is unable, or owing to such fear is unwilling to avail himself of the protection of that country; or who, not having a nationality and being outside the country of his former habitual residence as a result of such events is unable, or, owing to such fear, is unwilling to return to it. (Geneva Convention in Tuitt 1996, 12)

Central to this legal definition is the concept of alienage (being from elsewhere) and transborder mobility. You cannot be an internal refugee. As

Tuitt has argued, law uses the transborder mobility of the refugee to construct a limited definition and therefore limited obligations for host nations.

> Transborder movement – as an identifying feature of the phenomenon of refugeehood – is clearly at odds with images of the very young who lack the basic sustenance to move beyond that required for elementary functions. The concept of alienage, at its most basic level of understanding, is separate from the reality that drought, famine and similar causes of human suffering, by their nature immobilise large sections of the population, particularly the young and vulnerable and those upon whom they depend. (Tuitt 1996, 12–13)

By limiting the definition of refugee to those who are able to move the perception of refugees in the host country focused on a population determined by their ability to move – a population that is overwhelmingly adult and male.

The movement of refugees from one state to another poses a question of the moral and legal use of sovereign power of states to admit aliens into their territory. As people-without-place, refugees represent a crisis point in state power. The appearance of refugees and asylum-seekers in the United Kingdom, for instance, has been met with repressive and reactionary calls to protect "our place" against the alleged "flood" of incomers who, it is said do not "belong" here. One reaction – the 1996 Asylum and Immigration Act sought to counter the non place-specific intent of the Geneva Convention by producing a White List of countries that were deemed to be safe. Anyone claiming asylum from these places could then be automatically refused based purely on the place they originated.

Reactions to refugees and asylum-seekers in the press and by government officials from both major political parties are full of metaphors of fluidity. Allen White has commented on the story circulating in 2001 that asylum-seekers and illegal immigrants had introduced the foot and mouth virus into the United Kingdom's herd of cattle. It is a story, he argues, that matches the intense pathologization of refugees, asylum-seekers and immigrant in general.

> In the UK, hydraulic metaphors imagine flows of migrants (water, blood, diseases) leaving and entering states (reservoirs, lake or the body) that are protected by international borders and immigration laws (dams or surgical instruments). Flows may be "out-of-control" threatening the livelihoods of

all citizens, thus "floods" of refugees or asylum-seekers threaten to "swamp" the state. Representing the state and refugee movements in such a simplistic, but seductively holisitic, way legitimates the replacement of polyvocal, complex and chaotic stories and realities of migrant life with a monochrome universe of truth. (White 2002, 1055)

These metaphors of fluidity have a long and controversial history in the United Kingdom. Peter Jackson traces some of the history of these metaphors noting how they were used by the government minister, Enoch Powell in speeches about immigration in the 1960s, Margaret Thatcher in her 1979 election bid and in the press at the time of the introduction of compulsory visas for visitors to Britain from some parts of the non-white Commonwealth in 1986. The *Sun* headline read "3,000 Asians flood Britain" while the *Daily Express* read "Asian flood swamps airport" (Jackson 1989, 143–144). Despite the outrage expressed each time these metaphors have been used they have become even more prevalent in the 1990s and beyond as the moral panic about refugees and asylum-seekers has risen to new heights. The *Daily Telegraph* of 27 October 1995, for instance, read "Asylum Seekers: Dutch stem the flood of illegal immigrants" (*Daily Telegraph*, 27 October 1995). Government ministers frequently talk of the "rising tide" of asylum applications and speak of "flood gates" being blown asunder. These metaphors are "out-of-place" metaphors. They insinuate that place, boundaries (floodgates) and stability are under siege from the fluid and mobile refugees. Not only are the refugees and asylum-seekers from other places but they supposedly threaten "our place" and "our culture."

The image of the refugee and asylum-seeker in Britain has been heavily racialized. Refugees are conflated with different races in the argument that accepting more in the country will threaten internal race relations. In these arguments the focus is invariably on non-white refugees. The focus on the racial/ethnic origins of refugees diverts attention from the reasons for migration and promotes the view that refugee control is in fact control of "economic migrants." It is easier to make a case against people labeled economic migrants than refugees. Refugees are also criminalized. They are accused of wholesale fraudulent transactions with social security and more recently a direct connection has been drawn between refugees and terrorists. This has led to compulsory fingerprinting of all applicants for asylum regardless of evidence, the holding of asylum-seekers in detention centers and discriminatory housing law. As long as people without place are treated as criminals they will probably be seen as criminals.

So called "new asylum-seekers" – mostly non-white people who are engaged in inter-continental travel – are a post 1970 phenomenon. These new asylum-seekers (new, that is, to the Western world) challenged the previous "white" image of refugees fostered by the convention which was drawn up with reference to white Europeans. It is these people – non-white asylum-seekers who are often described as "bogus" or "economic migrants." Language such as this continues the process of constructing the refugee as a problem and as a threat to "our place." In addition, once they get here, they are said to take away resources which rightly belong to "our" people:

> What gives *the asylum problem* particular urgency is the growing scale of the abuse of the system…By abusing [asylum], people from abroad with no legitimate claim to be here can fend off removal and secure a prolonged stay, during which they can work in the black economy and take advantage of a range of public services and benefits. (Ann Widdecombe quoted in Young 1997, 64)

What the reaction to refugees, asylum-seekers and immigrants in general reveals is the way of thinking and acting that Malkki calls "sedentarist" – a view of the world that values roots, place and order over mobility and fluidity. This leads us to think of mobile people as disruptive and morally suspicious. Place thus plays many roles in the construction of the refugee. At a metaphysical level it leads to suspicion of the mobile. At a legal level it makes the definition of the refugee possible. As a matter of history the construction of places called nations made the existence of the refugee as foreigner a possibility in the first place.

Animals Out-of-Place

Places (and homes) are not just human. From the outset we have seen how places are gatherings, or assemblages, of material things (walls, trees, roads etc.), meanings (stories, narratives, ideologies) and practices (the many things we do). Included in these assemblages are other living things – plants and animals. What we decide to include in place, and what, conversely, we decide to banish from place, tells us a lot about how places are being constructed. Here I focus on animals. If we think of a home in the UK or USA – we might expect to find a cat – a domestic pet. A cat (assuming it was not a lion or a jaguar) would not seem out-of-place. Having a cat in domestic space would be unlikely in the home of a gypsy-traveler however. The anthropologist, Judith Okely has described how gypsy-travelers do not generally approve of having pets, especially cats, inside the home. They see them as sources of pollution disrupting the purity of interior-space. The idea of a cat licking milk from a saucer that might be used by a human is quite disgusting to them (Okely 1983).

Today, in most Western cities, we would be surprised to find a horse tied up outside a restaurant. One hundred and twenty years ago horses were extremely common in cities – US cities were practically built on the power of horses (McShane and Tarr 2007). The animals we might expect to encounter in urban places are geographically variable. Western visitors to India are often shocked to encounter water-buffalo on the streets as they make their way from the airport into the center of Delhi. Five million fowl share urban space with people (and other animals) in Dakar, Senagal (Hovorka 2008). Part of the process of defining places has been the gradual shifting of what animals belong and which are considered transgressive.

Animals play a key role in the production of urban place. Alice Hovorka has shown how chickens have played a central role in the urban landscape of Greater Gaborone, Botswana. Her account is framed within a general observation that the presence of animals in cities has not been a major focus of work in urban studies.

> African cities are fully populated with nonhuman dwellers. The presence of livestock in urban Africa may be attributed to economic circumstances of human dwellers given rapid urbanization, as well as enabling political scenarios and sociocultural identity tied to agrarian tradition. Yet urban livestock have snuck under academic and policy radars largely because they are out-of-place. Not only are livestock not supposed to be in cities, they are not readily visible given their placement in or preference for out-of-the-way spaces and temporary use of land across the urban landscape. (Hovorka 2008, 95)

One way to interpret my highlighting of the presence of livestock in the cities of Africa or India is to focus on the alleged backwardness of these heterogeneous regions. The presence of certain kinds of animals (livestock) in certain kinds of places (cities) can be seen as a measure of development or modernity. When a country wants to appear as "modern" or "developed" on the world stage there are often stories of the removal of animals from highly visible urban spaces. This happened recently in the Winter Olympics in Sochi, Russia, as stray dogs were removed from urban space.

A dog shelter backed by a Russian billionaire is engaged in a frantic last-ditch effort to save hundreds of strays facing a death sentence before the Winter Olympics begin here.

Already, hundreds of animals have been killed, with the local authorities apparently wanting the stray dogs cleared from the streets before Friday's opening ceremony.

While the authorities say the dogs can be wild and dangerous, reports of their systematic slaughter by a pest removal company hired by the government in recent months have outraged animal rights advocates and cast a gruesome specter over the traditionally cheery atmosphere of the Games. (Herszenhorn 2014, A1)

The presence of either livestock or wild animals in urban settings frequently upsets expectations about what belongs where. The presence of foxes in suburban London is the subject of periodic moral panics – as is the presence of coyotes in US cities. Where I lived until recently, in West London, I was frequently greeted by gaggles of bright green parakeets flying from tree to tree. In 2009 a suggestion was made that these birds needed to be culled as they were presenting a danger to "native" species. This is how it was reported in *The Guardian*.

English Nature has announced that from January, ring-necked parakeets' protected status will be removed so landowners can shoot or poison them without first obtaining a licence. This cull, said one environmentalist, was "racism" against exotic immigrants. While they originated in the Himalayas and only came here as pets, parakeets, added the London Wildlife Trust, were now "as British as curry." ...

Parakeets are crevice-nesting birds. They make their nests early in the year and choose holes in tree trunks favoured by native species, including great and lesser spotted woodpeckers, owls and willow tits. Some conservationists fear that with such rapid expansion they are out-competing and, possibly, eradicating rare native birds by nabbing their nesting sites as well as their food, rather like the aggressive alien grey squirrel has decimated populations of the native red in the last two centuries. (Parkham 2009)

To label a species as "native" is to suggest that it belongs – that it is in-place. Species such as the parakeets are labeled "alien invasive species" and are frequently met with hostility. Native species are thought to be inherently good while alien species are thought to be inherently bad. If you expand the time frame far enough it becomes almost impossible to tell whether a

Figure 6.2 A ringnecked parakeet on a bird feeder in Bromley, London, UK.
Source: photo by tiny_packages (originally posted to Flickr as Garden Parakeet)
[CC-BY-2.0 (http://creativecommons.org/licenses/by/2.0)], via Wikimedia Commons.

species is native or not – hence the claim that the parakeet is as "British as
curry."

Animal geographers have pointed out that often it is the case that one
species that has arrived relatively recently to a place is humans (Wolch
2002, Power 2009). Emma Power interviewed peri-urban residents in Australia to explore how their sense of home was ruptured or otherwise by the
presence of possums in their gardens and, often, in their homes. To some
they represented an unwelcome intrusion into home-space. Others,
however, recognized that this was the possums' home place and that they,
the humans, were actually the intruders.

Participants' encounters with possums were framed by discussions about whether possums belonged, or did not belong in the urban and urban-bushland environments that participants lived in. Participants' beliefs about whether possums belonged in these environments shaped their own sense of hominess in these spaces and in the house-as-home. Although urban environments have traditionally been framed as human-only-spaces, participants expressed a more complex conception of possum-belonging that drew on narratives of nativeness, invasion, colonialism and contemporary urban development. (Power 2009, 38)

We share our places, however urban, with animals. Sometimes we are welcoming and sometimes we are not. Accounting for the ways in which animals are welcomed or, alternatively, labeled "out-of-place" is a telling component in the analysis of place-creation.

Conclusions

In this chapter we examined the role of place in the constitution of the normal and the "pathological" – the "in-place" and the "out-of-place." We saw how various conceptions of place and place as home played an active role in the constitution of the normal, the natural and the appropriate and how deviation from the expected relationship between place and practice led to labels of abnormality and inappropriateness. Here place is used to construct the taken-for-granted world. The homeless are not simply people without a roof over the head but people who are evaluated as being in the wrong place (the city, the country, outside, in public). Refugees are not simply people who are moving to escape persecution but people who are constituted by their displacement. LGBTQ people are seen as "out-of-place" because they disturb the heteronormative character of many of the places that surround us. Animals are characterized as belonging or not belonging depending on the degree to which they fit into our conceptions of what a nation, a city or a domestic home (for instance) should be like as a place.

Writing about and researching place involves a multi-faceted understanding of the coming together of the physical world (both "natural" and "cultural"), the processes of meaning production and the practices of power that mark relations between social groups. The production of meaningful worlds in contexts of asymmetrical power relations occurs at all scales across the globe – from putting a poster on the wall to declaring a new nation. Places are co-produced by the people that constitute "society," all manner of living things, material objects, stories and practices. At the same time they are key to the production of relations between people and between people and other animate and inanimate things. Place, in other words, is right at the center of humanity.

Place appears in one form or another in a remarkably diverse array of research and writing across academic disciplines as well as in the practices of artists, architects and other. What this book has shown is that when reading research that evokes place it is important to analyze how the writer is using place as a way of looking at the world. We have also seen how "place" is not just a conceptual tool of geographers and other academics. It appears daily in our newspapers, in the pronouncements of politicians and in the social world that surrounds us. The furniture store tells us we can turn space into place; the real estate business tells us what kind of place we should want to live in; politicians and newspaper editors tell us that certain people or animals are "out-of-place." Artists and writers attempt to evoke place in their work and architects try to literally create a sense of place in their buildings. "Place," then, is not the sole property of geographers or even of academics. Place is constantly evoked in the world at large and has an extraordinary impact on the way in which people, animals, and all manner of things are represented and treated. The power of place can be felt at all scales from the corner of a domestic worker's room to the way in which we imagine the whole earth. It is difficult to object to the philosopher Jeff Malpas's view that place is one of the most important interdisciplinary concepts for the twenty-first century.

References

Anderson, K. (1991) *Vancouver's Chinatown: Racial Discourse in Canada, 1875– 1980*. Montreal, McGill-Queen's University Press.

Bauman, Z. (1995) *Life in Fragments: Essays in Postmodern Morality*. Oxford, Blackwell.

Bell, D., Binnie, J., Cream, J. and Valentine, G. (1994) All hyped up and no place to go. *Gender, Place and Culture* 1, 31–47.

Bell, D. and Valentine, G. (1995) *Mapping Desire: Geographies of Sexualities*. London and New York, Routledge.

Brown, M. P. (2000) *Closet Space: Geographies of Metaphor From the Body To the Globe*. London and New York, Routledge.

Cloke, P., Milbourne, P., and Widdowfield, R. (2000) Homelessness and rurality: "out-of-place" in purified space? *Environment and Planning D: Society and Space* 18, 715–735.

Craddock, S. (2000) *City of Plagues: Disease, Poverty, and Deviance in San Francisco*. Minneapolis, University of Minnesota Press.

Cresswell, T. (1994) Putting women in their place: The carnival at Greenham Common. *Antipode* 26, 35–58.

Cresswell, T. (1996) *In Place/Out of Place: Geography, Ideology and Transgression*. Minneapolis, University of Minnesota Press.

Cresswell, T. (2001) *The Tramp in America*. London, Reaktion.

Deutsche, R. (1988) Uneven development: Public art in New York City. *October* 47, 3–52.

Douglas, M. (1966) *Purity and Danger; An Analysis of Concepts of Pollution and Taboo*. New York, Praeger.

Duncan, N. (1996) Renegotiating gender and sexuality in public and private spaces, in *BodySpace*, ed. N. Duncan, London, Routledge, pp. 127–145.

Halfacree, K. (1996) Out of place in the country: Travellers and the "rural idyll." *Antipode* 28, 42–72.

Herszenhorn, D. M. (2014) Racing to save dogs roaming around Sochi. *New York Times*, 6 February, p. A1.

Hovorka, A. (2008) Transspecies urban theory: Chickens in an African city. *Cultural Geographies* 15, 95–117.

Hubbard, P. (1997) Red-light districts and toleration zones: Geographies of female street prostitution in England and Wales. *Area* 29, 129–140.

Hubbard, P. (1998) Community action and the displacement of street prostitution: Evidence from British cities. *Geoforum* 29, 269–286.

Hubbard, P. (2000) Desire/disgust: Mapping the moral contours of heterosexuality. *Progress in Human Geography* 24, 191–217.

Jackson, P. (1989) *Maps of Meaning*. London, Unwin Hyman.

Kitchin, R. (1998) "Out of place," "knowing one's place": Space, power and the exclusion of disabled people. *Disability and Society* 13, 343–356.

Malkki, L. (1992) National geographic: The rooting of peoples and the territorialization of national identity among scholars and refugees. *Cultural Anthropology* 7, 24–44.

May, J. (2000) Of nomads and vagrants: Single homelessness and narratives of home as place. *Environment and Planning D: Society and Space* 18, 737–759.

McShane, C. and Tarr, J. A. (2007) *The Horse in the City: Living Machines in the Nineteenth Century*. Baltimore, Md, Johns Hopkins University Press.

Okely, J. (1983) *The Traveller-Gypsies*, Cambridge, Cambridge University Press.

Parkham, P. 2009. Is it time to start culling parakeets? *The Guardian*, 12 October. Online. Available at www.theguardian.com/environment/2009/oct/12/ring-necked-parakeet-cull (acessed 9 May 2014).

Parr, H. and Philo, C. (1995) Mapping mad identities, in *Mapping the Subject*, ed. S. Pile and N. Thrift. London, Routledge, pp. 199–225.

Philo, C. (1987) "The same and the other": On geographies, madness and outsiders. Occasional Paper 11, Loughborough University of Technology, Department of Geography.

Philo, C. (1992) The child in the city. *Journal of Rural Studies* 8, 193–207.

Philo, C. (1995) Animals, geography, and the city: Notes on inclusions and exclusions. *Environment and Planning D: Society and Space* 13, 655–681.

Power, E. R. (2009) Border-processes and homemaking: Encounters with possums in suburban Australian homes. *Cultural Geographies* 16, 29–54.

Sassen, S. (1999) *Guests and Aliens*. New York, New Press.

Sibley, D. (1981) *Outsiders in Urban Societies*. New York, St. Martin's Press.

Smith, N. (1996) *The New Urban Frontier: Gentrification and the Revanchist City*. London and New York, Routledge.

Tuan, Y.-F. (1991) A view of geography. *Geographical Review* 81, 99–107.

Tuitt, P. (1996) *False Images: Law's Construction of the Refugee*. London, Pluto Press.

Valentine, G. (1993) (Hetero)sexing space: Lesbian perspectives and experiences of everyday spaces. *Environment and Planning D: Society and Space* 11, 395–413.

Valentine, G. (1997) Angels and devils: Moral landscapes of childhood. *Environment and Planning D: Society and Space* 14, 581–599.

Veness, A. (1992) Home and homelessness in the United States; Changing ideals and realities. *Environment and Planning D: Society and Space* 10, 445–468.

White, A. (2002) Geographies of asylum, legal knowledge and legal practices. *Political Geography* 21, 1055–1073.

Wolch, J. R. (2002) Anima urbis. *Progress in Human Geography* 26, 721–742.

Young, C. (1997) Political representation of geography and place in the United Kingdom Asylum and Immigration Bill (1995). *Urban Geography* 18, 62–73.

7

Place Resources

When it comes to place, life is fieldwork. The world itself is the best kind of resource for thinking about place. A lot can be learned from reflection on everyday experience. Notice how, in Chapter 4, Doreen Massey develops her approach to place by walking down her local high street. Similarly, David Harvey reflects on the newspaper accounts of a local area that he may have read over breakfast. Pick up a newspaper and there are place stories in it. Place not only surrounds us but is a key ingredient in many of the media through which we indirectly experience the world – the Internet, newspapers, film, music, and literature. This chapter, however, focuses on more specialized resources for work on place. The most obvious resource, of course, is the literature on place from within the diverse disciplines that tackle place issues. This chapter introduces the key texts. In addition it indicates some useful web resources and suggests some projects on place.

Key Books on Place

The literature that uses place is endless. The following is a list of some of the key books (single authored and edited) that have taken place as a central concept. Many of them have been mentioned in this book. The list is organized by discipline but starts with geography, as that is the discipline I approach the world from.

Place: An Introduction, Second Edition. Tim Cresswell.
© 2015 John Wiley & Sons, Ltd. Published 2015 by John Wiley & Sons, Ltd.

Anthropology

Augé, Marc (1995) *Non-Places: Introduction to an Anthropology of Supermodernity.* London, Verso.

A widely read extended essay on the way in which old ideas of place as deeply rooted, authentic centers of meaning have been challenged by the increasing pro- liferation of places of movement and travel. Written from the perspective of a French anthropologist.

Feld, Steven, and Basso, Keith, eds. (1997) *Senses of Place.* Washington DC, School of American Research Press.

A compelling collection of eight in-depth ethnographic essays exploring the ways in which place is imagined and experienced by diverse groups of people around the world.

Low, Setha, and Lawrence-Zuniga, Denise, eds. (2002) *The Anthropology of Space and Place: A Reader.* Oxford, Blackwell.

A collection of key essays from the discipline of anthropology that take space and place as important concepts for issues of human culture and identity.

Tsing, Anna (2005) *Friction: An Ethnography of Global Connection.* Princeton NJ, Princeton University Press.

An increasingly influential account about how the particularity of actually exist- ing places influences the circulation of supposed "universal" phenomena such as capital, science, and political ideologies. Place is not the central concept but the book is, nevertheless, about how place continues to matter in a globalized world.

Architecture

Alexander, Christopher, Ishikawa, Sara, and Silverstein, Max (1977) *A Pattern Language: Towns, Buildings, Construction.* New York, Oxford University Press.

While Alexander is something of a maverick in the world of architecture, his account of the way patterns make places at all scales is enormously influential with architects seeking to consider the "spirit of place" in their building projects.

Day, Christopher (1993) *Places of the Soul: Architecture and Environmental Design as a Healing Art.* London, Aquarian/Thorsons.

Christopher Day follows an approach to architecture informed by the teachings of Rudolf Steiner. The idea of holistic and healthy place is central to Day's writings and practice. He believes that buildings should induce well-being by being good places to be in.

Dovey, Kim (1999) *Framing Places: Mediating Power in Built Form*. London, Routledge.

Dovey, Kim (2010) *Becoming Places: Urbanism/Architecture/Identity/Power*. London, Routledge.

Kim Dovey is an Australian writer on architecture. His writing stands out for its attention to the way building involves the idea of place. *Becoming Places* is a particularly clear engagement with assemblage theory and includes a series of examples of building projects to illustrate the assembling of place (quite literally).

Norberg-Schulz, Christian (1980) *Genius Loci: Towards a Phenomenology of Architecture*. London, Academy Editions.

Norberg-Schulz, Christian (2000) *Architecture: Presence, Language and Place*. London, Thames and Hudson.

Christian Norberg-Schulz is both a practicing architect and a writer on architecture and place. His development of the classical idea of *genius loci* reveals a close attention to the idea of local place in the process of making buildings.

Art

Dean, Tacita (2005) *Place*. London, Thames & Hudson.

An exhibition in a book. Dean gathers art that asks questions of the place of place in the world. Art which ranges from the natural world to busy city streets is presented in the context of a visual discussion of the ways in which place shapes and influences us.

Doherty, Claire (2004) *Contemporary Art: From Studio to Situation*. London, Black Dog Publishing.

A series of essays, interviews, and case studies of the many ways in which artists engage with place from the studio to the gallery to the broader world outside. Collectively the book examines the important roles place plays in the production of art as well as asking how art can help us think about place.

Kwon, Miwon (2004) *One Place after Another: Site-Specific Art and Locational Identity*. Cambridge, Mass., MIT Press.

An influential account of site-specific art from its emergence in the 1960s to the conceptual and critical art of the turn of the twentieth century. This includes a typology of ways in which art relates to site from phenomenological attempts to fit into the "spirit of place" to critical attempts to connect places as sites of art across the globe.

Lippard, Lucy (1997) *The Lure of the Local: Senses of Place in a Multicentered Society*. New York, New York Press.

Lippard is a writer on art and culture who turns her attention to place and the local in this book. Her aim is to use art to think through the senses of place that emerge in a multi-cultural society.

Creative non-fiction

There has been a lively resurgence in forms of creative non-fiction that deal with issues of place ranging from "nature" writing to urban psychogeography. In many cases there is a very definite attempt to "re-enchant" place. The following are some good examples.

De Leeuw, Sarah (2004) *Unmarked: Landscapes along Highway 16*. Edmonton, NeWest Books.

Evans, Gareth, and Robson, Di, eds. (2010) *Towards Re-enchantment: Place and Its Meanings*. London, Artevents.

Farley, Paul and Roberts, Michael Symmons (2011) *Edgelands*. London, Random House.

Macfarlane, Robert (2008) *The Wild Places*. London, Penguin.

Sinclair, Iain (2009) *Hackney, That Rose-Red Empire*. London, Penguin.

Solnit, Rebecca (2013) *Faraway Nearby*. London, Penguin.

History

Hayden, Delores (1995) *The Power of Place: Urban Landscapes as Public History*. Cambridge Mass., MIT Press.

A very accessible and suggestive account of the role that place plays in the production of history, heritage, and memory in a number of urban landscapes.

Turkel, William J. (2007) *The Archive of Place: Unearthing the Pasts of the Chilcotin Plateau*. Vancouver, University of British Columbia Press.

This book is a detailed investigation of the Chilcotin Plateau in British Columbia, Canada. In addition to exploring a place through archives in libraries and museums, Turkel considers what happens when we think of the place itself as an archive full of information for those who know how to look for it.

Media studies

Couldry, Nick (2002) *The Place of Media Power: Pilgrims and Witnesses of the Media Age*. London, Routledge.

Couldry's book considers the continuing importance of non-mediated place in the way that news stories are constructed. The focus is on what happens when people who are used to viewing media suddenly find themselves to be the objects of media attention. This draws our attention to the places where media happens – the site of a news story or a film location for instance.

Meyrowitz, Joshua (1985) *No Sense of Place: The Impact of Electronic Media on Social Behavior*. New York, Oxford University Press.
    Meyrowitz argues that electronic media (particularly television) are producing an increasingly placeless world where experience is constantly mediated and homogenized. Should be read alongside Relph and Augé.

Moores, Shaun (2012) *Media, Place and Mobility*. Basingstoke, Palgrave Macmillan.
    This book focuses on the ways in which media can be used to make places in everyday life. Moores is particularly attentive to the way we use mobile technologies, such as mobile phones, to enact a phenomenological act of dwelling in the modern world.

Philosophy

Bachelard, Gaston (1994) *The Poetics of Space*. Boston, Beacon Press.
    An extremely influential book mixing psychoanalytic theory and phenomenology to explore the meanings of particular kinds of space, drawing on the experience of the interior of a house. This does not mention place particularly but is, nevertheless, about the way space is imbued with meaning.

Casey, Edward (1993) *Getting Back into Place: Toward a Renewed Understanding of the Place-World*. Bloomington, Indiana University Press.
Casey, Edward (1998) *The Fate of Place: A Philosophical History*. Berkeley, University of California Press.
Casey, Edward (2005) *Representing Place: Landscape Painting and Maps*. Minneapolis, University of Minnesota Press.
    This trio of books by the philosopher, Edward Casey, seeks to understand why place has been relatively neglected by philosophers. The books consider the different ways in which philosophers have thought about (or ignored) place in their work and makes a carefully argued case for the importance of place. The earliest book is the more accessible but the last of them is the most "applied" – featuring the role of place in the world of art and cartography.

Malpas, Jeff E. (1999) *Place and Experience: A Philosophical Topography*. Cambridge, Cambridge University Press.
Malpas, Jeff E. (2006) *Heidegger's Topology: Being, Place, World*. Cambridge, Mass., Harvard University Press.
    A rich and sophisticated attempt by a philosopher, over two books, to locate place at the center of considerations of human experience as well as at the center

These books and papers explore the role of place in the production and reproduction of memory and heritage in various contexts.

Atkinson, David (2007) Kitsch geographies and the everyday spaces of social memory. *Environment and Planning A* 39, 521–540.

Charlesworth, Andrew (1994) Contesting places of memory: The case of Auschwitz. *Environment and Planning D: Society and Space* 12, 579–93.

Cooke, Steven (2000) Negotiating memory and identity: The Hyde Park Holocaust Memorial, London. *Journal of Historical Geography* 26, 449–465.

Cresswell, Tim, and Hoskins, Gareth (2008) Place, persistence and practice: Evaluating historical significance at Angel Island, San Francisco, and Maxwell Street, Chicago. *Annals of the Association of American Geographers* 98, 392–413.

Delyser, Dydia (2005) *Ramona Memories: Tourism and the Shaping of Southern California*. Minneapolis, University of Minnesota Press.

Desilvey, Caitlin (2007) Salvage memory: Constellating material histories on a hardscrabble homestead, *cultural geographies* 14, 401–424.

Edensor, Tim (2005) *Industrial Ruins: Spaces, Aesthetics, and Materiality*. Oxford and New York, Berg.

Foote, Kenneth E. (1997) *Shadowed Ground: America's Landscapes of Violence and Tragedy*. Austin, University of Texas Press.

Hayden, Dolores (1995) *The Power of Place: Urban Landscapes as Public History*. Cambridge, Mass., MIT Press.

Hornstein, Shelley (2011) *Losing Site: Architecture, Memory and Place*. Farnham, Ashgate.

Hoskins, Gareth (2007) Materialising memory at Angel Island Immigration Station, San Francisco. *Environment and Planning A* 32, 437–455.

Johnson, N. C. (1996) Where geography and history meet: Heritage tourism and the big house in Ireland. *Annals of the Association of American Geographers* 86, 551–566.

Lowenthal, David (1996) *The Heritage Crusade and the Spoils of History*. London, Viking.

Neville, Brian, and Villeneuve, Johanne (2002) *Waste-Site Stories: The Recycling of Memory*. Albany, State University of New York Press.

Nora, Pierre, and Kritzman, Lawrence D. (1996) *Realms of Memory: Rethinking the French Past*. New York, Columbia University Press.

Till, Karen E. (2005) *The New Berlin: Memory, Politics, Place*. Minneapolis, University of Minnesota Press.

Place, cyberspace, information technology

In the last decade there has been an enormous growth in the ways we can interact with, and augment, place through the use of information technologies. We can do this through our computers, our mobile phones, and (soon) through our glasses. The challenges this poses to thinking about place represent an important research agenda for the twenty-first century. These readings represent a starting point.

Crang, Mike, Crang, Phil, and May, Jon, eds. (1999) *Virtual Geographies: Bodies, Space and Relations*. London, Routledge.

McCullough, M. (2013) On the nature of attention, with ambient interfaces at street level. *Continuum: Journal of Media and Cultural Studies* 27, 505–513.

Mitchell, William J. (1995) *City of Bits: Space, Place, and the Infobahn*. Cambridge, Mass., MIT Press.

Mitchell, William J. (2003) *Me++: The Cyborg Self and the Networked City*. Cambridge, Mass., MIT Press.

Wilken, Rowan, and Goggin, Gerard, eds. (2012) *Mobile Technology and Place*. New York, Routledge.

Zook, M. A. and Graham, M. (2007a) The creative reconstruction of the Internet: Google and the privatization of cyberspace and DigiPlace. *Geoforum* 38, 1322–1343.

Zook, M. A. and Graham, M. (2007b) Mapping DigiPlace: Geocoded Internet data and the representation of place. *Environment and Planning B: Planning and Design* 34, 466–482.

Place, ecology, the environment

One important strand of writing on place has focused on the environment and ecology. Because places are weaves or gatherings of varied elements, the idea of place presents an opportunity for holistic thinking about sustainability and ethical living. Here places are conceived of as a tight connection between regions and their resources, flora and fauna. Often a "natural" foundation, such as a watershed, is given as a basis for thinking about places in this way. The following are some key examples of this tradition.

Berthold-Bond, Daniel (2000) The ethics of "place": Reflections on bioregionalism. *Environmental Ethics* 22(1), 5–24.

Jackson, Wes (1994) *Becoming Native to This Place*. Lexington, University Press of Kentucky.

Norton, B. G. and Hannon, B. (1997) Environmental values: A place-based theory. *Environmental Ethics* 19(3), 227–245.

Sale, Kirkpatrick (1985) *Dwellers in the Land: The Bioregional Vision*. San Francisco, Sierra Club Books.

Smith, Mick (2001) *An Ethics of Place: Radical Ecology, Postmodernity, and Social Theory*. Albany, State University of New York Press.

Snyder, Gary (1995) *A Place in Space: Ethics, Aesthetics, and Watersheds: New and Selected Prose*. Washington, DC, Counterpoint.

Spretnak, Charlene (1997) *The Resurgence of the Real: Body, Nature and Place in a Hypermodern World*. Reading, Mass., Addison-Wesley.

Thayer, Robert L. (2003) *LifePlace: Bioregional Thought and Practice*. Berkeley, University of California Press.

Key Journals

The most up-to-date writing on place can be found in specialist academic journals centered on the discipline of geography. Regularly checking on these journals will enable you to see how the concept of place continues to evolve and how researchers and writers use the concept in different, often competing, ways. The list is limited to journals printed in English.

ACME
Annals of the Association of American Geographers
Area
Australian Geographer
Canadian Geographer
Geoforum
Geography Compass
Geografiska Annaler Series B
New Zealand Geographer
The Professional Geographer
Transactions of the Institute of British Geographers

These journals all cover the broad range of geography, both human and physical, and are often the main publication outlets for national geographical societies. They are considered leading places to publish work that speaks to international audiences.

Antipode: A Radical Journal of Geography
This journal focuses on work that links academic inquiry to social and political change and activism. Work is normally informed by radical theoretical traditions such as Marxism, feminism, and anarchism.

cultural geogaphies
Social and Cultural Geography

Cultural geography is one of the subfields that has had most to say about the idea of place and landscape. These journals frequently deal with the construction and maintenance of places as well as challenges posed to them. The papers in *cultural geographies* tend to be a little more theoretical and humanities based while *Social and Cultural Geography* is more social science based and applied.

Environment and Planning D: Society and Space

Papers in this journal tend to be more theoretically focused than in other journals, It is usually a place to find "cutting-edge" developments in the field.

Ethics, Place and Environment

Here papers focus on ethical issues within geography and beyond. These include environmental ethics and the role of place in the construction of "moral geographies."

Gender, Place and Culture

Papers here focus on the interrelations between gender, sexuality, and geography. It is the major outlet for geographers informed and inspired by feminism.

Health and Place

This journal, unsurprisingly, focuses on the interrelations between health and medicine, on the one hand, and place, on the other. You can expect to see work here on healthy and unhealthy places, contagion, historical beliefs about disease and space, etc.

Journal of Historical Geography

This is where to look for in-depth articles on places in the past as well as on the role place plays in the constructions of memory and heritage.

Political Geography

This journal deals with the interrelations between geographical worlds (including place) and various levels of politics from the formal and institutional to the more everyday variety. A good place to look for work on boundaries, the nation, regional governance, etc.

Progress in Human Geography

This is an excellent place to read reviews of geography's various subfields and papers which attempt to summarize developments in the field and suggest innovative ways forward.

of memories that are not being reproduced in these places. Why is this? Places are not just small scale and local. Nations are places too. How are nations constructed in relation to selective histories? How are the indigenous peoples in North America, Australia, New Zealand, or Taiwan (for instance) represented or hidden in discussions of the nation? You might consider the production of selective histories around a major sporting event such as an Olympics opening ceremony.

Practice and place

How are practice and place connected? How does the repitition of everyday activities produce a particular sense of place? How are places constructed to encourage some forms of practice and discourage others?

It is necessary to get beyond consideration of the material form of places and representations of them in order to fully comprehend the complexity of place. The things that people (along with things, animals, plants, etc.) do can never be fully predicted and the best-laid plans are often transformed by the stubborn repetition of practice. How is your place practiced? What forms of repetition can be observed that produce a unique kind of "place-ballet"? How does a place change through the day? What are its rhythmic geographies? What kinds of practice disturb these repetitions? A lot of work on practice will be about mundane practices of everyday life and this is sometimes difficult to write about and research because it is so unremarkable. Careful observation will be necessary for such projects.

Place and politics

How do politicians promote places through the creation of national territory? What representational strategies are used to create political places from the local to the global? How do processes of internationalization on the one hand, and devolution on the other, create a new landscape of places?

Place is important to politicians. Politicians from the local council to the United Nations want to encourage a sense of belonging and citizenship. In order to do this they have created communities of people that feel as though they "belong" to a place. Since the eighteenth century, politicians have been creating the place of the nation-state through such strategies as the conferral of citizenship rights, national anthems, passports, creation myths, and monumental spaces. More recently regional politicians have sought to promote particular images of region-as-place. In the UK, this has become important in places such as Wales and, particularly, Scotland. In the USA, states have consistently fought with the federal government over the allegiance of citizens, Texas is a good example of this. On another level, some places in the USA have been promoted as liberal places to live by their local politicians – think of West Hollywood or Vermont. Finally, politicians on an international scale have sought to produce places that subsume or supersede, nations. The European Union is an obvious example.

Place, protest, and resistance

How are places used in political protest? What kinds of places do forms of protest produce? How are the material landscape, representations and practices subverted by political groups?

Recently we have seen how Occupy protestors drew attention to themselves by both occupying already existing places in cities around the world and producing their own kinds of places in the tent cities – complete with restaurants, child-care, and universities. Similar processes have occurred in major revolutionary movements such as that which occurred in Tahrir Square in Cairo or Independence Square in Kiev. There is a long history of this kind of place-subversion including the barricades of the Paris Commune (1871) or the long history of marches in Trafalgar Square in London. Places provide symbolic resonance for protests. And there are also less spectacular and more everyday forms of resistance and rebellion in which places are reconfigured. Examples include graffiti, squatting, skateboarding, parkour, urban exploration, and yarn-bombing.

Index

Place: An Introduction, Second Edition. Tim Cresswell.
© 2015 John Wiley & Sons, Ltd. Published 2015 by John Wiley & Sons, Ltd.